Seasons, Species & Patterns of a North East Atlantic Rocky Shore

(A Research and Photographic Journey through Time and Space at Ross Beach, Loophead, Co. Clare, Mid-Western Irish Coastline)

Carmel T. Madigan

First published in 2014 by:
The Loophead Summer Hedge School
Kilballyowen, Loophead,
County Clare, Ireland

Facebook: The Loophead Summer Hedge School
Web: www.carmelmadigangallery.com

ISBN:978-0-9572127-1-8

A copy of this book has been lodged for cataloguing with the British Library and with Trinity College, Dublin.

Graphic Design & Layout - Carmel T. Madigan
Printed & Bound in Ireland

A Loophead Summer Hedge School Publication funded by the Madigan Family

CONTENTS PAGE

FOREWORD *Matt Murphy*

Carmel's family history with the Loophead Peninsula stretches back at least ten generations, through a long line of mostly fishermen and coastal farmers. Growing up on the coast Carmel has always felt a strong link with the sea and Ross Beach in particular. She recalls early morning trips to the shoreline to collect driftwood with her siblings and father and how Sundays were days for nature walks with her mother. This, and further exploration on her own, instilled a passion that continues today.

I first learned about the rich marine and plant life of the Loophead Peninsula from James, Carmel's youngest son. For the past few years James has entered our annual competition for primary school children in Munster. The depth of the projects, especially from one so young, have always been impressive, making him a worthy winner on many occasions. Through James I got to know his mother Carmel and soon realised where James' passion for nature came. A professional artist, Carmel's first book "The Wild Flowers of Loophead" was published in 2012, illustrating her artist flair and love of colour and place. Now in this book Carmel has "married" this creativity with her love and understanding of the seashore habitats of Ross Beach.

Ireland has an extremely rich coastline and the wealth of marine life from the high tide mark to the low water often goes unnoticed. Carmel's indepth study of this one beach highlights not only the prolific and complex marine life on Ross Beach but her indepth study can serve as a tool for those wanting to research other shores around our coastline.

One cannot but be impressed with Carmel's enthusiasm for her subject, which comes across in every page. The numerous photographs of marine animals and seaweeds bring the book to life and Carmel's easily accessible text guides the reader gently through the seasons and lifecycles of species on the shore. It is an incredible record in time for Ross Beach and Carmel should be very proud of her achievement.

Although Carmel tells us it took five years to research, in reality the seed was sown much earlier, when as a child she explored Ross Beach. She is fortunate to have a son whose curiosity with nature rekindled her love of the place near where she grew up and ultimately resulted in this fine book.

Matt Murphy

Director, Sherkin Island Marine Station

May 2014

FOREWORD *Master James Madigan*

Carmel Madigan is my mother. It is very inspiring for a son to see his mother reach these heights. Creating a book for people to enjoy, following thousands of hours of demanding work. It makes you feel that this is the right way to work, to put the head down and really try hard, and for many it works in the end. This is a great example to show where hard work brings you. As the son of the author, you get great behind the scenes access to what she does, and you really see the passion that drives her. Every time I go home from school the first thing I hear is the exciting news from Carmel about her trip to the rocky shore of Ross Beach earlier that day, it draws you in. It makes you excited. There is an ecstatic feeling with her, it just comes out, the love, the passion, all the positive emotions. It's great to come home to that.

This book is all about these feelings, even read through some pages of this book and you'll get the hint of excitement in it. It makes you want to explore yourself. After years of sore feet walking around the jagged, rough rocks of Ross Beach, this is her work. I must say myself, I'm very impressed with it. It justifies the tremendous work that she had to go through to make this book alone, forget the 5 years of studying new found seaweeds, periwinkles and other bits and bobs you discover on this very interesting shore. Even going through all the winter storms, getting drenched many times, some falls on slippery rocks (especially me) she loved it. I loved my time on the shore studying with her too. It wasn't all serious, we had lots of fun, slipped in and broke a good camera, lost the car keys to the ocean.. and more.. Not one complaint. I think it is this attitude that should be enjoyed in this book, and even though this book is only concerned with the rocky shore and the sea, I think everyone should realise that this book is a great example of hard work and passion.

So I wish every reader of this brilliant book, enjoyment, celebration, appreciation and first and foremost, insightful learning.

James Madigan
Rice College, Ennis
Barefield National School
May 2014

Reflective Gull - Mid-Summer, at Ross Beach, Loophead.

1 INTRODUCTION

Ross Beach has existed on the remote, isolated, windswept Loophead Peninsula on the Mid-Western Irish coast for millions of years. Its coastal address is that of the North East Atlantic Ocean. Here this small north west facing inlet brings a tiny segment of the Atlantic to its final destination at its eastern edge. Always moving inward or outward, even when appearing motionless, the ocean is the single most important natural element affecting the community that hug its boundary. Of course there is more than one community hugging its boundary. On the one hand, there are the farmers, fishermen, small businesses, tourist operators, professionals and diverse creative community being influenced by the Atlantic ocean here in the course of their daily lives. On another level there is the vast and even more diverse community, that of the inter-tidal community that occupy the small band of territory between land and sea and who are swarmed directly by the ocean each day. For this community, the ocean is the provider: provider of water, nutrient, refreshment, opportunity, shelter. It filters through their daily lives and unlike the terrestrial community, they cannot exist without it.

This book came about as a direct result of a self-empowered journey of exploration. Using a myriad of resources ranging from the valuable simplicity of wellingtons, magnifying glasses, wind breakers, caps, clear plastic containers, rubber gloves to the more sophisticated underwater digital camera, the internet, books and a significant stock of commissioned reports and ecological studies. I dug deep into the lifestyles, living patterns, needs and requirements of shoreline inhabitants. This took time. On the one hand setting out with only a miniscule of knowledge, I firstly needed to search for and locate the living creatures and plants bounding the shoreline. I then needed to name them. With so many hiding places, so many tiny creatures, so many different creatures and so many plants, this took time. I needed to understand the tidal patterns, the safety issues, I needed company, another set of eyes, I needed to watch out for seasonal variations, tiny changes from one visit to the next, semblances of reproduction and methods of reproduction. In the end it was a determined investigation to 'crack' the beach code of Ross Beach.

One may enquire as to the driving forces and purpose of this particular journey lasting in excess of five consecutive years. The answer is audible in our ancestral footprints. Our family's history is immersed in this coastline habitat. Stretching back at least ten generations, and possibly many more, our people were fishermen, coastal farmers and victims of the ocean. My great grand-father Denis Liddane was drowned while Currach fishing off Tullig, whilst my great grand-aunt, Kate Gorman a young girl of seventeen years was drowned when cut off by tides while harvesting seaweeds at the Goleen near Tullig. This was a scene of extreme sadness, as the locals and the parish priest stood helplessly by, as she finally slipped off the rock into the tide. My siblings John Paul and Kevin Magner became lighthouse keepers, spending time and sharing experiences from many rock, island and shore based lighthouses around the coast of Ireland. They, together with my brother Patrick and my father PJ, were casual fishermen, fishing for Lobsters, Crabs, Crayfish, Mackerel, Pollock. In addition John Paul was a scuba diver, aiding in the retrieval of artifacts from the Movern amongst other adventures. He had also scuba dived at Ross beach. My parents, Mai and PJ Magner yearned and valued some of the produce of the beach, most especially Dillisk (Sea Grass), Carrigeen, Bárnachs and Sliochán. I was on occasion a rocky shore forager, belting the Barnáchs off their sturdy holding on the rocks for our dinner on Fridays.

At a deeper level, each of us connected with Ross beach every day. There were the early morning trips to the shoreline by my father before the cows were milked. Timber poles (driftwood) may have been washed up. This was always collected, left higher on the shore, above the tide line, if it was too heavy and wet for one person to carry. My father and mother new the comings and goings of the beach like clockwork. The calendar that hung on our wall had to have the moon cycles. With this they were able to monitor the highest and lowest tides. We listened to its sounds, decibels ranged from near silent to extremely loud roaring. Living so close, we were guaranteed this range of sound day and night. With strong northern gales, encouraged by the ocean, my father had to re-enforce our front door on a regular basis over the Winter months, lest it blow in. Then there were the rough Spring tides flattening the loose shingle mound that was its perimeter and natural wall. This meant no access for days, maybe weeks to our local shops, church and school. On a lighter note, my siblings and I collected shells for school and home craft work, we swam in a tiny sandy cove, monitored the cormorants on an outer rock. On Sundays, my mother and I took long nature walks along the coastline, collecting the odd bag of mushrooms from the adjacent moorland, and observing the tiny flora, which were nameless to us. Finally, we could not access our Church – the Church of the Little Ark, our primary and secondary schools, our community hall for sports and concerts without encountering Ross Beach. Cycling by the beach in the dark, was at best, hair raising. Ocean sounds are exponentially more ominous in the dark. During evening masses in the Wintertime, my mother armed with a hand lamp for light ensured she had our company on her journey to the church past the beach.

It is perhaps evident from the foregoing, that this self empowered beach research project, is indeed a natural move on my behalf given our association and interactions with the beach. Having been almost completely disconnected for decades, my return was immediately filled with excitement and a sense of intimacy. Being separated by decades, didn't matter, it felt like I had never been away. With grown up eyes, it suddenly became a true journey of enlightenment of appreciation and understanding. The things I never saw, the things I never knew, now resplendent and familiar. A deep bond of intimacy formed, as surefootedness developed with every shore trip, a welcome for me who wanted to come, explore, enjoy, enlighten, share the knowledge and beauty of this isolated, lonely place. This re-connection with the beach was facilitated by James, my young son, who wanted to investigate it for a Sherkin Island Marine Project, having stumbled upon it during the course of our wildflower research of the beach shingle. Our combined monitoring, research and enjoyment became our very own Institution, and it will remain so. This is the journey of a lifetime.

Being on the edge of the mighty Atlantic Ocean at Ross, ones imagination is likely to stretch and radiate. What and who may be at the other side of the Atlantic at this latitude? Who is looking this way, but can't see us, like we can't see them. To the western edges of the North Atlantic ocean at this level there is Canada's provinces of Newfoundland and Labrador. At the same Northern latitude as Ross, there is the tiny Canadian coastal town of King's Cove, on the Bonavista Peninsula on mainland Canada's east coast. With a population of just one hundred and twenty one (2006), mainly Irish settlers, fishing, forestry and mining are the main occupations of its residents. Names like Murphy, McGrath, Barrett, Carew and Walsh abound. I am fascinated, for on reading more I find that the Bonavista Peninsula approx. 3000kms away, feels more Irish than Loophead itself.   I wanted to know more about our next door neighbours directly across the pond. The following is a quick environmental and social overview of both locations.

Western Atlantic
(Bonavista Peninsula)

Eastern Atlantic
(Loophead Peninsula)

Above: An iron lighthouse erected in1893 on the scantily populated Bonvista Peninsula headland on the rugged granite coastline of the province of Labrador /Newfoundland in mainland Canada.

Above: Loophead Lighthouse, together with lighthouse keepers quarters on the Loophead Peninsula was built of stone in 1854 on the most westerly tip of the rugged mainly sandstone/slate/shale coastline of West Clare.

Bonavista Peninsula

Above: Images of the rocky coastline of the Bonavista Peninsula, conjure up similarity with our own in terms of beauty and rugged layers. There is a high granite and iron content in these formations. This is an ancient formation from the Precambrian period 500million years ago.

Ross Beach

Above: Ross Beach Loophead, a low lying sandstone, slate and shale rugged formation dating back to the Namurian era 300 million years ago.

Kings Cove

Bounding sheltered inlets in this much fragmented eastern Canadian coastline, an abundance of wood from the dense forests which survive here to the detriment of most other vegetation, meant that early settlers built their homes with wood. At Loophead the presence of wood may best be found at Ross Beach as beached escapees from Canadian forest felling. No trees survive the bleak and blustery Loophead landscape.

Western Atlantic
(Bonavista Peninsula)

Eastern Atlantic
(Loophead Peninsula)

Above: A young graveyard of a community that was first established in 1690 by James Aylward from Co. Cork. His descendants still live here.

Above: Timpeall na Naoi Néamh - Ross a place of ancient monastic settlement and saints dating back to the fifth century. Saints such as St. Cúan spent time here.

Flour and provisions in this remote area of Kings Cove were difficult to come by. Winters could produce snowfalls of up to 120 inches and accessibility wasn't always possible. Flour was generally traded for fish. Fishing companies came and went, sometimes leaving the fishermen unpaid. It was sometimes necessary for five or six men to trundle eighteen miles to another town for a barrel of yellow corn meal, and haul it through snow-Banks with ropes over their shoulders. Nonetheless they had plenty of Herring. Many settlers from Cork and Kerry only spoke Irish. Settlers from Wexford spoke English.

Land was barren, rocky, moss covered rock at the edge of tundra and agriculture was not supported or encouraged until the 1960's when the village was suffering and losing its population.

Bought provisions including tea, flour and sugar, were provided for three generations by Bonfil's Shop just beyond Ross Beach. Many domestic food supplies were cultivated from tillage, fishing, poultry and bacon.

At Ross, land is arable, and farms were self-subsistent growing a wide range of crops, dairy farming,and using the produce of the sea and shore. Like the rest of our nation, there were periods when our crops failed and the land was tenanted, not owned. At these times, access to Ross beach was limited to the paid up tenants of the local landlord, Mr. Wesby who owned the beach and assigned its use for the cultivation of seaweed and other food in plots to his tenants. This system prevailed during the Great Famine. Seaweed was regularly drawn from the beach to condition and enrich the soil during and after this era. Right: A traditional Ross farming homestead - adjacent to Ross Beach.

In this reverie, this stretch of the imagination to wonder what may exist on the other side, I find myself intoxicated by the comparisons, differences and similarities between the two communities flanking the Atlantic Ocean at equal latitude but differing orientations. The most striking finding was to unearth a community here that was an almost entirely Irish community.

However vast differences exist, not only at the physical level, but even more so at the climatic level. What makes Loophead vary so much in its climatic conditions from that of Kings Cove in mid-Winter for example? According to worldweatheronline.com average temperatures for Kings Cove range from zero to minus ten degrees Celsius for six months of the year from November through to April, never reaching a peak above 21 degrees Celsius during the Summer months. According to Met Eireann - met.ie 'The moderating influence of the Atlantic is felt throughout Ireland..... Although our inland stations show more variation, there is only about one day or less per year when the air temperature stays below freezing point. Minimum air temperature falls below zero on about 40 days per year at the inland stations, but on less than 10 days per year in most coastal areas. Air temperatures inland normally reach 18 to 20 °C during summer days, and about 8°C during wintertime'. In a nutshell the Atlantic Ocean is dragging warm water currents and airflows upwards and eastwards across 7000kms of ocean surface from the Gulf of Mexico. This is known as the Gulf Stream. These warm water currents are merging with warm water airflow currents from America's east coast - The North Atlantic Drift, and we are therefore being 'warmed' very significantly by two warm water currents. Meanwhile, Canada's Labrador Coastline is being chilled by the Cold Labrador Current, moving southwards from the Artic Circle.

At Kings Cove, Labrador Newfoundland, temperatures are typically sub-zero for six months of the year. Given our identical latitudes, it is startling to discover such climatic variation.

At Loophead, average Winter temperatures of 8 degrees Celsius, with temperatures dipping below zero along the Irish Coastline for less than ten days per annum.

The significance of the eastern Atlantic ocean accompanied by its warm currents becomes very evident. The Atlantic ocean gifts the Irish coast with a moderate, temperate climate. This in turn supports a wide array of livelihoods, especially farming, tillage, and other growth forms. Perhaps, like some shore flora and fauna, we too may not be able to survive without the warm lashings of the Atlantic. During the course of this book, we will meet its important contributions and powerfulness time and again. In this context the Atlantic ocean provides the backdrop, to every creature and seaweed that I will introduce in the next chapters. It comes to the forefront however, in my final chapter 'Pulse Events - An Ocean in flux and at War'. An unplanned chapter, brings to the fore its uncontrollable powers, its power over our territory, livelihoods, lives.

Ross Beach, Loophead is on the Wild Atlantic Way situated at 52 35 10 53 N and - 9 52 12 92 W.

MAPS

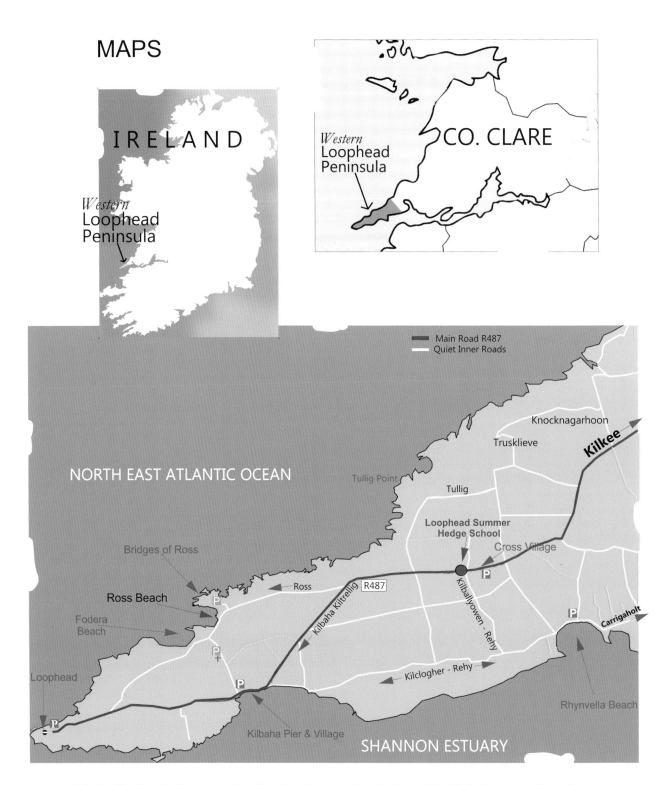

WESTERN LOOPHEAD PENINSULA

Ross Beach, Loophead is on the Wild Atlantic Way situated at 52 35 10 53 N and - 9 52 12 92 W.

2 CREATING STARTING POINTS

The rocky shore is a very distinctive habitat, one that scientists have rewarded with a very specialized vocubulary. My aim throughout this book, is to keep scientific terminology to a minimum, as the rocky shore is quite an intriguing place, that moves well beyond that of categorization, classification, survey and analysis. Of course scientific knowledge feeds well into the spectre of understanding, and identification, and garnering a sense of who is related to who and so forth. However, without being burdened with the requirement to classify and box and scientifically describe the behavioural activities of the shore, the lightness of observation of specie and action for all its glory, the fascination with nature for all its wondrous diversity, the evolvement of a sense of connection, the delight of being present, will all immensely enrich the being. The shore is a place of magnificent beauty, of change and seasonal variation, of courage, bravery, strategy, hiding, babies, regeneration, reproduction, living. Viewing the rocky shore in this way, is like unlocking the drama of life itself.

In my subsequent chapters, I keep categorization to a minimal. I look at the creatures here as a group of inhabitants, the inhabitants of Ross Beach, and the seaweeds, lichens and flora for their diverse, edible, useful and commercial interest, their behaviour and beauty.

Certain pieces of scientific knowledge will greatly assist with ones understanding of the rocky shoreline. This makes it easier for the explorer eager to find and look at some creatures, easier to locate seaweeds and making ones trip to the shore safer. Therefore as well as introducing a glossary of terms that will be found throughout this book, I also aim to show how the beach may be zoned for interpretation purposes, show what many particular micro habitats may look like (this is not exhaustive), present the lunar cycle of Spring and Neap tides, and present a rocky shore safety code for newcomers to this wonderful but potentially dangerous habitat. With this knowledge studied, the newcomer to the rocky shore will be well prepared for some wonderful excursions and days out on the coastline. Of course, one may also book a guided educational tour to the shore with me, directly to Ross Beach, Loophead, Mid-Western Irish Coast, the scene for the research of this book! I run these tours regularly during Spring Tides, especially over the Summer Months. During the school year I take primary and secondary school pupils on educational tours to Ross beach.

Considerations & Planning for Field Trips

- Obtain times of Low Spring Tides for your area- Tide Tables - (*available printed media - internet*).
- Don't go alone.
- Take your mobile phone.
- Wear suitable footwear - rocky/slippy/wet - I use wellingtons (*crude but great!*).
- Always carry light rain gear and head gear.
- Backpack allows for hands free movement.
- Always follow an outgoing tide and lead an incoming tide.
- Be aware of changes in the ocean - faster water flow, louder sounds etc.
- Monitor safe and quick exits from your location on shore.
- Be light footed and avoid trampling on heavily occupied areas.
- Respect shore creatures - this is their home.
- If you turn over a stone to look beneath, return it to former position.
- Do not remove creatures for pets - they will not survive.
- Move slowly and observe closely for best experience.
- Take notes and images to cherish.

Glossary of Rocky Shore Terminology

Alginic Acid - an insoluble gelatinous carbohydrate found (chiefly as salts) in many brown seaweeds. The sodium salt is used as a thickener in foods and many other materials.

Aqua-culture - Cultivation of sea life for commercial purposes.

Assemblage - Community of organisms living in a specific habitat.

Asexual Reproduction - Reproduction methods where no recombination of genetic material occurs.

Beach - Strip of land along the margin of a body of water, that is washed by waves generally interpreted as referring to sediment, mobile boulders rather than bedrock shores.

Bedrock - A stable hard substratum that is not segmented into boulders.

Benthic - Refers to organisms attached to or living on the sea bed.

Bio-luminesence - The light-making abilities of certain creatures using chemical proteins.

Bio-mass - The total quantity of living organisms in a living area.

Biota - The plant and animal life of a particular site.

Bivalve - A shell consisting of two calcareous valves joined together by a flexible ligament.

Boulder - An unattached rock.

Brackish - Refers to mixtures of saltwater and freshwater.

Brooding - The incubation of eggs - inside or outside the body. Males or females may be responsible for brooding.

Bryozoa - Grouping of simple sessile creatures made up of small individuals called zooids - encrusting sheets or mats.

Budding - Form of asexual reproduction, where a new individual begins life as an outgrowth of a parent. May be colony forming or independent.

Calcareous - Chalky - containing calcium carbonate.

Carnivore - A predator which feeds on animals.

Carrageenans - Are food additives derived from red seaweed such as *Chondrus crispus* (Irish moss) and other species and are used as a thickening, stabilizing, and texturizing agents in foods and also for reduced-fat meat products

Cirri - Slender hair-like filaments used during feeding.

Cnidaria - An animal group where each member has stinging tentacles e.g Anemones and Jellyfish.

Colony - A group of organisms of the same species, living together in a common mass.

Community - group of organisms occurring in a particular environment.

Crevice - A narrow crack in a hard substratum less than 1cm wide.

Crustose - Forming or resembling a crust.

Cryptic - an animal which lives in hidden places, or an organism whose appearance or colouration makes it difficult to see and recognise.

Current - A steady flow of water in a particular direction . Current refers to the residual flow after any tidal element has been removed.

Desiccation - Removal of water, the process of drying out.

Detritus - Fragmented particles - organic matter - decomposition of plant and animal.

Direct Development - Development without a larval stage.

Ebb-tide - Going out or falling tide.

Ecology - Study of inter-relationships between living organisms and their environment.

Ecosystem - A community of organisms and their physical environment, inter-acting as a unit. (Can be used at a macro or micro level).

Glossary of Rocky Shore Terminology

Encrusting - Coating with a thin crust.

Epibiotic - Living attached to the surface of another organism, without any detriment or benefit to the host.

Epiphytic - Growing on the surface of a living plant (but not parasitic).

Fecundity - Potential reproductive capacity of organisms or population.

Foliose - Bearing leaf-like structures.

Frond - Leaf-like structure of a seaweed.

Gastropod - Mollusc snail that crawls on its foot.

Grazers - Animals which rasp algae.

Habitat - A place in which an animal or plant lives.

Herbivores - Organisms which feed on plants.

Hermaphrodite - Having both male and female reproductive organs.

Holdfast - A root-like structure that attaches seaweed to substratum, but has no nutrient gathering role.

Hydroid - A stinging animal, related to Anemones and jellyfish.

Intertidal Zone - The space between highest and lowest tides.

Iridescence - Showing luminous colours which seem to change with viewing angle.

Juvenile - Life between larval and adult stage - with the absence of reproductive ability.

Kelp - A large brown algal grouping.

Kelp Forest - A belt of Kelp sufficiently dense to form a canopy.

Larvae - An early phase in an organism's life-cycle.

Latitude - An angular distance measured in degrees north or south of the Equator.

Longitudinal Fission - Asexual reproduction method where one animal tears itself into two animals, e.g Dahlia Anemone.

Lunar Tidal Cycle - Tides governed by astrology. (Sun & Moon).

Migration - Movement from one region or habitat to another.

Moderately Exposed - Generally coasts facing away from prevailing winds, but where strong winds can be frequent.

Neap tide - The lunar tide of minimum range occuring at the first quarters and third quarters of the moon.

North East Atlantic - Stretch from the North Cape to the Straits of Gibraltar excluding the Baltic.

Omnivores - Organisms who have a mixed diet of plant and animal.

Pelagic - Creatures living entirely at sea.

Predator - An organism that feeds by preying on other organisms - killing them for food.

Recruitment - Term used for the addition of a young new individual to a population.

Regeneration - Replacement by growing back, that which has been lost - e.g arm, frond etc.

Salinity - Measure of the concentration of dissolved salts in seawater.

Salt marsh - Areas of peat & other deposits almost permanently wet and frequently inundated with saline waters.

Scavenger - Any organism that feeds on dead organic material.

Sedentary - Attached to a substratum, but capable of some movement around it.

Sediment - Grains of solid material accumulated by natural processes.

Glossary of Rocky Shore Terminology

Seasonal - Showing periodic changes in line with seasons.

Sessile - Permanently attached to a substratum.

Shingle - Beach pebbles normally well rounded as a result of abrasion.

Shore - The land along the edge of a body of water.

Splash Zone - The zone above the high tide mark that gets splashed by ocean spray.

Spring Tide - The Lunar tide of maximum range, occurring at just after new or full moon.

Sub-tidal - A term for the seabed below the mark of lowest Spring tide.

Succession - Sequential development of plant and animal communities through time.

Symbiosis - The living together in a constant and definite relationship of two different organisms.

Scour - The effect of abrasion usually by sand or gravel on the seabed.

Strandline - A line on the shore comprising debris deposited by a receding tide.

Thallus - A plant or lichen body looking like true leaves, stem and root.

Translucent - Allows light to pass through without being transparent.

Zooid - An individual animal connected together in a common mass constituting a colony.

Zooplankton - The animal component of plankton.

Ross Exposed Coastline

Anemone - Sea Creature

Seaweeds
Plants of the Sea

Simple explanation of the Lunar Cycle & Tidal Pattern

You may wonder why I wish to write about astronomy in this book.. in a nutshell Astrology controls the Lunar tides. These are the pattern forming tide cycles that play out on the shore each month. Each twenty eight days a new cycle commences.

The Moon circulates the earth all the time. It takes twenty eight days to perform this circulation. The earth has magnetic powers within the solar system. The sun is the other main player. The sun too has magnetic powers over the moon and the earth. Sometimes the Sun, Moon and Earth are in a straight line. This happens twice a month, New Moon and Full Moon, fourteen days apart. This is depicted in Diagram 1. When this happens the Sun is pulling at its strongest on the moon which in turn has a stronger pull on the earths surface because of this. This causes bulges on the earths oceans. These bulges cause high and low **Spring Tides**. A low Spring tide is much lower than any other tide. The water disappears off the beach. Then the tide turns, meaning that at a particular point (normally six hours from start of withdrawal), it begins to return again. For six hours it will be returning at various velocities and reaching much further up the shore than at any other time (excepting special events). This means that a Spring tide is not only the lowest tide but it is also the highest tide. As the Moon moves around the earth at an approx daily movement of 12degrees, the main effects of a Spring tide will last approx two to three days at either side of a New Moon or a Full Moon.

So what happens when the Moon, moves away from its direct line with the Sun and therefore away from its magnetic pressure? The tidal bulges on the oceans surface return to normal, so the bulges disappear, so that by the time of the 1st quarter seven days after a New Moon, the Moon and Sun are at right angles to each other. On the surface of the ocean, this plays out with a tide that withdraws very little over a period of six hours and returns very little over a period of six hours (excepting special events). In other words, there is very little difference between low tide and high tide during this period. This is called **Neap tide**.(Diagram 2).

It is very important that when visiting the rocky shoreline to browse and explore, that one is aware of the tidal pattern of the day. Being familiar with the Lunar cycle is critical, and these can be found online, in some calendars and in various publications such as tide tables. Once one is aware of the Lunar Cycle, and the tide times for a particular day, it is very possible to plan a useful exploration trip. Ecologists and naturalists the world over prefer to visit the rocky shore during periods of Low Spring Tide. Low Spring Tide uncovers the lowest part of the shore together with its living organisms and it will provide for the most interesting trip at the lowest levels. Of course, at higher vertical levels on the shore, there will be rock pools exposed for greater lengths of time during any tide. These too provide for fantastic explorations.

Furthermore, there are twenty four hours during which the tide is continually moving in one direction or another. The tide typically takes six hours to withdraw (**ebb tide**), and six hours to return (**flow tide**) every single day. That's just twelve hours. So each single twenty four hours, it performs this cycle twice. This is called the **day/night cycle** or **diurnal cycle.**

It may be fascinating to note at this point, that many shore creatures are internally clocked with the tidal rhythms, that determine critical factors, like when to eat, and when to reproduce. For instance, crabs generally hide during day time under rocks - hiding from predators such as gulls and oystercatchers. and at night time high tides move up and down the shore predating their wide selection of prey. Sub-tidal fish move up shore during night time high tides. Birds, will wait until day time low tides, when they can see and catch their prey. Limpets too, prefer night time high tides, remaining fastened to rock during day time low tides to prevent predation, especially from birds.

Understanding such factors greatly enhance the shore visit, whether your aim is to disprove a theory, discover a new strategy, or simply enjoy being in the midst of such marine industry.

The Lunar Cycle

Diagram 1

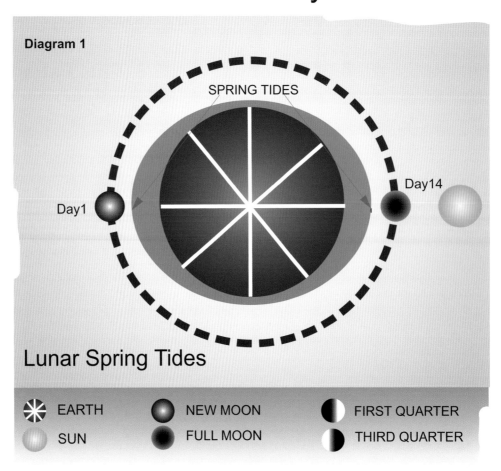

SPRING TIDES

Day1

Day14

Lunar Spring Tides

| | EARTH | | NEW MOON | | FIRST QUARTER |
| | SUN | | FULL MOON | | THIRD QUARTER |

Diagram 2

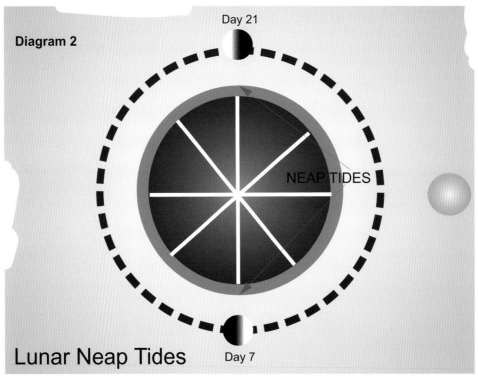

Day 21

NEAP TIDES

Lunar Neap Tides

Day 7

Lunar Cycle = 28 Day Cycle = 12deg. change per day

On the shore - Low tides look like these

Low Spring Tide

Every two weeks

Low Neap tide

Every two weeks

On the shore - Incoming High Spring/Neap Tides look like these

Above - An incoming Spring tide. This one will reach right up to the top of the shore to the level shown at (1). This is the line of organic debris that is left behind by the tide at the end of its inward journey. This tide is somewhat driven by strong northern winds but not storm. Below, a much lower incoming Neap Tide finalizes itself much lower on the beach leaving its strandline of organic debris as a reference as seen at (2). Note also a calmer day.

Zoning Ross Beach - Inter-tidal Zones

The Atlantic rocky shore at Ross, is a temperate climate rocky shore in North West Europe. It is a compact shore with a short inlet that is north facing, and leads in from a very exposed outer coastline with constant breaking waves against the vertical cliffs and outcrops. This inner shore could be described as relatively sheltered or moderately exposed. At both sides of this short inlet there are rocky shore formations consisting of bedrock, boulder, shingle and sediment. There are gentle vertical gradients within this shore, and a wide span of rock surface. With creatures so small, many measuring only 5mm or less, species so varied, and time generating constant change, it was a great idea for scientists to look at the shore from a broader perspective. Of course one cannot form a broader perspective, unless one has closely studied all the fine detail. Over time, all over rocky shores throughout the world, it became apparent, that conditions such as continuous access to ocean water, or very little access to ocean water, well lit spaces, rocky substrata, rock pool, linkages with another specie, all became dominating factors, in the general positioning of all shore organisms. Thus within any vertical gradient on the shore, which controls access to ocean water, a community of organisms had settled that found that gradient particularly suitable to them. Above this gradient, some may still survive and below this level more still survive, as there are no clean lines in such wild spaces as rocky shores. Images presented a 'banding' effect especially on steep sloping rocky shores, and the process of **Inter-tidal Zonation** began in earnest.

The Inter-tidal Zone comprises of compartments of a rocky shore that range from just being sprayed by ocean mist to being continuously submerged i.e the complete area from the top of the shore to the shallow sub-tidal, is known as the Inter-tidal Zone. Each zone is characterized by a banded colouration.

At the very top of the shore that evades all ocean water, except sea spray and an odd run over by a turbulent ocean, there is the '**Splash Zone**', the part of the beach that is coated by various lichens and an odd terrestrial plant in a crevice. It will be characterized by orange, yellow, soft green and soft grey hues.

Just below this section of the beach, there is a section that is characterized by a bright green seaweed, together with a couple of rock dwelling brown wrack seaweeds, that can sustain long periods out of water and also tolerate rainwater. These seaweeds have access to the least amount of ocean water, being the last to be covered with the rising incoming tide and the first to be exposed as the tide ebbs. This area is called the '**Upper Shore Zone**', and will appear, dark brown, bright green and black.

Further down the vertical gradient, one begins to meet with a band of heavily occupied barnacle coated rocks. At this level there are lots of gastropods, limpets, topshells and periwinkles grazing rock surfaces. Because of the dense barnacle settlement, the rock surface can appear dull beige/grey. This banded area is called the '**Middle Shore**' and is commonly referred to as the '**Barnacle Zone**'.

Further down the shore gradient, one begins to meet a whole combination of brown wracks, green and red seaweeds, and an increased amount of shore activity and a great competition for space amongst species. There are many encrusting species, including, seaweeds, sponges and other simple animals here too. Beneath boulders, there are crabs hiding. Birds forage here. This part of the shore receives the most coverage of incoming and outgoing tides, but it will be exposed twice daily. Welcome to the lively '**Lower Shore**'.

Beyond the lower shore, there is always water. This is the **Shallow-Sub-tidal Zone**, consisting of very rich eco-systems, that include the Kelp Forest - a dense forest made up of several species of very large brown seaweeds, often hosting a myriad of small fishes, egg masses, and epiphytic seaweeds.

On visiting the beach over a couple of occasions, it will become evident how neat this 'zonation' of the beach actually appears on the ground. It makes looking for species, identifying species and monitoring species all the easier, and I use this terminology right throughout my book, in describing organisms locations.

Ross beach is comprised of a gently sloping, widely splayed, vertical assent. The zonation banding within the beach are therefore quite wide. Some shores with sharp vertical drops, have a banding of creatures that is much more pronounced and could be viewed from a singular photograph. The gentle sloping of Ross beach provides a sense of ease when physically exploring the shore. There is a combination of rock types at play, the heavily textured shale being particularly comfortable for gripping.

■ Middle Shore Zone
■ Upper Shore Zone
▨ Splash Zone

UPPER ZONES OF ROSS BEACH

MIDDLE SHORE

UPPER SHORE

SPLASH ZONE

UPPER INTER-TIDAL & SPLASH ZONE

THE INTERTIDAL ZONE

LICHENS
PERIWINKLES

SPLASH ZONE

GUTWEED
CHANNEL WRACK
SPIRAL WRACK

UPPER SHORE

BARNACLES
GRAZING GASTROPODS
WHELKS
SMALL SEAWEEDS

MIDDLE SHORE

WRACKS
CARRIGEENS ETC.
ANEMONES
CRABS

LOWER SHORE

KELP FOREST

SUB-TIDAL

SHELTERED V EXPOSED

1 Exposed

2 Moderately Exposed

3 Exposed

Defining exposure level on a particular stretch of coastline may best be achieved by the non-scientist by relative comparison. On any given day trip, a comparison of a few adjacent stretches of coastline will provide enough evidence, to develop this relativity. The images on this page were taken on the same day on a small stretch of coastline. The images include Ross Beach itself (2), open coastline adjacent to the beach (1) and the next inlet just a couple of hundred metres away (3). There is a significant northern wind, and all locations are north west facing.

It is therefore possible to ascertain relative exposure. The north west facing open coastline (1) is extremely exposed, with constant vigorous bashing of rock by the ocean. Certain creatures and seaweeds enjoy this level of exposure and predation levels can be lower on extremely exposed shores. Sliocháin, the edible red seaweed, in particular thrives at exposed locations here. Ross Beach itself (2) is showing strong water movements, but there are little to no large breaking waves nearing the shore line. Meanwhile, the inlet adjacent to the Bridges of Ross (3) is in utter disarray, with huge incoming swells that land right onto the shoreline at low tide. All images have been taken within twenty minutes of each other. It becomes apparent that relative to the other sites photographed, Ross Beach itself can be described as moderately exposed or relatively sheltered. This therefore provides a platform and a habitat for all the particular seaweeds and creatures that prefer such an environment, generating a very rich bio-diversity at the beach.

Defining & Describing Habitats

'The area or environment where an organism or ecological community normally lives or occurs: a marine habitat.' *Dictionary Reference.com*

'*The marine environment supplies many kinds of habitats that support marine life. Marine life depends in some way on the saltwater that is in the sea (the term marine comes from the Latin mare, meaning sea or ocean). A habitat is an ecological or environmental area inhabited by one or more living species*' Wikipedia definition

I have been studying creatures and seaweeds on the shore over several years, paying particular heed to their location, their attachment structure, their vertical level, their access to elements such as light, salinity levels, cover, need to be constantly submerged and so forth.   It has been an intriguing exercise. On the one level, to generalize about any single creature is hazardous. There rarely are any clean lines of classification on the rocky shore. This is because it is a wild place with vast forces at play. Many times, I have attempted to generalize on movements, specific locations, specific changes, only to be presented with new evidence that negates the generalization. Remember this is a wild place full of energy, movements, forces.

In spite of this and given small margins of error, one finds amazingly concise classifications, patterns, locations, movements, seasonal variation, each little creature in its place, defining vertical lines of growth of a species, pool depth preference, coverage preference and so forth. Ross beach is full of 'code'. Cracking this code is akin to cracking all the habitats of the shore.

The shore is a maze of habitats. Here I describe a habitat as a sustaining location/position on which an organism lives, chooses to live and thrives in this position/ location. Habitats on the shore can range from the tiny to the expanse of the entire shore itself. It is important to consider some types of habitats, defined by their location on the shore and other environmental factors. This exercise focuses the eyes and attention on the small detail. As an artist, I thrive in the fine detail. The selection of habitats that I present here are just a miniscule of those available on the shore. I am working from small/micro habitats to medium and larger ones.

A selection of small habitats

The Topshell, albeit a moving gastropod, can provide a suitable hard substratum for encrusting seaweed species - especially *Ulva* species, Barnacles, Calcareous Tube Worms and more. Most live gastropod shells at various levels on the shore provide habitat, including Limpet shells, which host a different array of seaweeds and creatures, dependent on which vertical level on the shore one finds them.

The Seaweed frond - Seaweed fronds come in all shapes, colours, sizes and habitat. The Discoid Fork Weed is a year round seaweed growing in the shallow sub-tidal. It hosts creatures like Star Ascidians, egg masses, and Encrusting seaweed species. These are all organisms with a preference for the shallow sub-tidal. Most seaweed fronds, especially long life ones, throughout the shore host an array of sea life.

Calcified boulder

This was once a loose boulder located on the extreme lower shore. It could have been moved around the shore if turbulent ocean conditions prevailed. Overtime however, it has become re-attached to the substratum by calcification, so now it can't be moved out of position. It is probable that few, if any creatures can get in under it or live on its underside. However, it provides a stable habitat to lower shore sessile creatures and particular seaweeds who choose to populate, this type of surface.

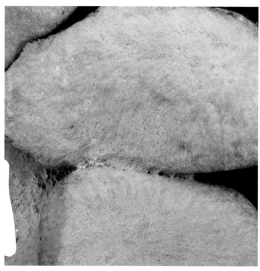

Well smoothed sandstone shingle, typically fronts the shore, and is typically the last part of the beach to be washed over and the first to be left exposed with outgoing tides. The combination of smoothness, openness to the direct light and lack of ocean coverage, means that most of this shingle remains unpopulated as a habitat. However at the lower part of the shore, one will find a distinct band - at average neap tide level, which is coated in green. A singular seaweed species can live at this lower level, on this smooth shingle and exposed to direct light.

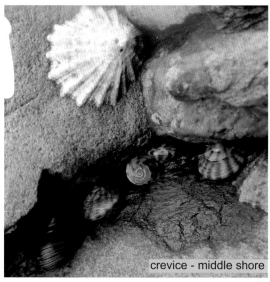

crevice - middle shore

A middle shore crevice is a great hiding place and safe haven for many juvenile gastropods. It is quite common to encounter mixed communities in these type of locations, many creatures between 5mm and 1cm in diameter. It is also a safe holding place during rough tides. When water moves over rock, it has least movement at the lowest level, so small creatures are generally undisturbed by turbulent oceans.

Above and beyond the lashings of the ocean but still in its salty spray filled environment, a splash zone crevice in bedrock, can provide enough collected soil for salt loving plants to extend their deep woody roots and survive bravely all the elements flung at them including many tidal run overs during rough Spring tides throughout the year. Because of its vertical level on the shore, however, gastropods could not survive here.

A selection of medium habitats

A much more significant habitat at Ross, is that of a Saltmarsh. This is an area above the tide line that is always waterlogged with brackish water that is sometimes run over by salt water. It is a place where Reeds and salt tolerant Rushes flourish together with a host of smaller plants and Red Fescue. Small birds, frequent it for feeding on insects. Most of the plants growing here assist in trapping and knitting soil together, providing terrestrial stability at the edge of the ocean. A distinctive multi-layered habitat.

Middle shore

The community of species that thrive in a shallow upper middle shore pool will vary very significantly with those that form a deep pool lower shore community. This pool has alot of broken shell gravel, which may be ideal for the likes of the Daisy Anemone, who likes to disappear beneath it when threatened. Lugworms will be happy to bury into the gravelly sand too. Prawns and Shrimps will enjoy it, especially in Summer and small species of seaweeds that enjoy full light will thrive here.

Lower shore

A deep rock pool on the lower shore. This medium sized habitat hosts community living. Seaweeds and creatures together occupying a specific space that is submerged by the ocean twice a day for a period of hours on each occasion. Being deep, with a largely shingle basin, it will not suit all sea life. It is fringed with bedrock and this provides a very suitable habitat for seaweeds and creatures, that prefer a more stable substrata. Ideal for large brown Wracks and Kelps and Encrusting species

The shallow sub-tidal - a very significant and important marine habitat always covered in sea water, supporting a huge community and diversity of sea life. Many organisms will only live when submerged in water all of the time. This is their habitat. Yet on an overall rocky shore habitat basis, it is just part of the story.

Community living

Shallow Pool Lower Shore

The shallow light filled pool in the bedrock substratum on the lower shore - So many creatures prefer the lower shore. Here they get to be washed over by the ocean for long periods of time twice a day. (Day-night cycle). In addition, many seaweeds prefer plenty of light to photosynthesize. Certain seaweeds will only grow and spread on hard rock (e.g encrusting - paint species). Predators such as anemones like the lower shore because it has more access to floating plankton and small fish. There is plenty grazing opportunity for gastropod herbivores like limpets, topshells and periwinkles, who will have their shells settled on with micro and macro algae.

A look at settlement spaces

Settlement surface space is the entire combination of bedrock, boulder, gravel, sediment, shingle, shell, seaweed, creature that form and populate the shore. The available surface space includes, moving, sessile, calcified and encrusted objects. Creatures and seaweeds choose their preferred settlement with much refinement, creating broad patterns of settlement amongst creatures, not only at vertical levels but also on preferred surface. This section presents a small selection of types of spaces available and what if anything may settle on such space.

Re-attached boulder on sheltered extreme lower shore cove. A popular habitat, a once smooth boulder heavily coated in seaweed coverage. Seaweeds generally will attach to a 'hard surface', therefore one will not find them attaching to anemones for example.

Smooth and loose lying sandstone boulders to the front of the shore in an exposed location. Not heavily sought after, yet populated with a bio-film sheen, which will provide grazing fodder for roaming limpets, periwinkles and topshells. Beadlet Anemones like this part of the shore because of the rich supply of tidal food.

A trickling salt water supply, through this smooth sandstone bedrock located on a sun facing position at the lower part of the middle shore. Pink Paint seaweed often colonizes such trickles.

Part of a fascinating rock formation above the tide line. A combination of sandstone and shale bedrock providing space for the settlement of lichens and insects.

The vertical gradient, creviced layers of this Namurian formation, presents an image of settlement patterns that will be covered throughout the book. At the upper end, there are the highest living lichens, beneath which are the highest living seaweeds, below which are the middle shore creatures and seaweeds. Ample space for hiding out in this heavily textured formation.

Sun facing textured bedrock with trickling water, provides a perfect space for this particular assemblage of Summer seaweeds on the middle shore. Limpets and certain Topshells can survive the heat and being out of water, by being clamped onto rock, or by sealing off the entrance to their shell to avoid dessication.

This weathered sandstone bedrock formation towards the upper shore has been settled on by Tar lichen. The holes provided by the weathering, will provide homes for creatures such as the Rough Periwinkle, the Small Periwinkle and small insects/worms.

Some of the available space at the front of the beach at a lower shore level, is that of free moving shell gravel and sand sediment. This provides poor settlement opportunity for seaweeds, but it provides burrowing, food and shelter for a wide range of creatures including the Lugworm.

Space but not much settlement. This attractive blue slate formation on the lower-middle shore, hosts a small quantity of Barnacles and a few lingering Limpets. It shows an under-utilization of space by both seaweed and creature at this part of the shore, which may be due to rock preferences or water flow/velocity into the sheltered cove or perhaps calcification issues with the slate.

Just below this formation, heavy Limpet occupation of an embedded sandstone boulder and serrated wrack settlement of sandstone boulder, depicts how uneven settlements can be throughout the shore.

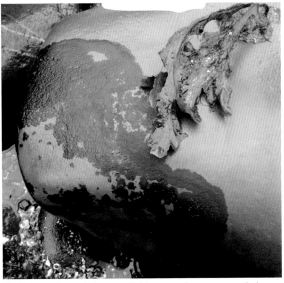

An interesting picture unfolds on a large smooth lower shore embedded boulder. The boulder has been settled on by a Tar Lichen. Obviously this Lichen is not very appetizing or is too difficult for the Limpet to graze on. Meanwhile the Limpet shell has been settled on by the macro algae, Bladderwrack and Ulva. Settling on the Limpet as opposed to the rock, means they cannot be grazed by the Limpet and will survive. The entire boulder is likely to be coated with Bladderwrack, if the Limpet wasn't present to graze its early settlement.

On the extreme lower shore, this significant tall boulder depicts that with the right prevailing conditions, space can be at a premium. The tall boulder also reflects on the gradient at which creatures and seaweeds settle in relation to each other.

3 ANIMAL LIFE ON THE ROCKY SHORE

Spotting animals on the rocky shore, can be fascinating. They are everywhere, occupying a wide variety of spaces and settlements, some hiding others in full view, some with adapted colourations that make them almost invisible, some brightly coloured, some well protected by heavy shells, others appearing much more vulnerable, some abundant, some scarce. Together as a group living on the small patch of shore that I have studied to produce this book, they present immense diversity - of form, function, food, of strategy, survival, space and settlement. Diversity and variation are the key words that describe not only the little creature itself but all its functions.

Some creatures are heavily preyed on. You may think these ones are not the ones with the shell protection, but the soft bodied creatures. This is not the case. Shelled gastropods can be cracked open, smashed open, or have their inhabitant dragged out by the narrow pincer claws of the Velvet Swimming Crab. Crows for instance will take a Dogwhelk off the shore and fly to a higher cliff location where they will drop it a few metres onto a rock ledge, to split open the shell. Shells do not guarantee safety on the rocky shore, but they certainly assist, and they assist the inhabitant when being bashed about by the ocean, hitting off one rock and then another.

Where do animals hide from rough oceans? Bearing in mind the significant rough ocean storms of the Winter just past (2014), it was uplifting to note, that the populations of most shelled creatures seemed none the worse for its tantrums. This observation is based on the fact that I have been continuously monitoring the shore, its populations and creatures for the past five years. So the day after the roughest of oceans, with the vast decimation of the Kelp Forest for instance, I am so happy to note it is business as usual for the tiniest juvenile gastropods, in the crevices, on open rock, grazing. During rough ocean storms a couple of factors are evident. Firstly the water speed at the floor level of the water column is the slowest, and most of the time its movement is barely noticeable, while the surface water has the highest velocity. Secondly, creatures sense the ocean turbulence and hide in crevices, on the sheltered sides of rocks, beneath rocks and so forth. Creatures such as the Common Shore Crab have already left the shore during Winter. However, no rock is safe during ocean storms, being liable to be hurtled across the beach and landed well beyond its zone. So the best place to hide is in the crevices of very significant re-attached boulders and in the crevices of bedrock.

Many soft body animals like small fishes and worms fall prey to a whole host of predators on the shore. There are the terrestrial predators, mostly birds, and there are the shore predators, crabs, anemones, whelks and many others. As aforementioned many shell protected creatures also fall prey to these predators. Large and well populated creatures like Limpets are grazers. They eat algal spores - the seedlings of new seaweed. In this way they keep rocks clean of seaweed, but sometimes it grows on top of their shell, where it is relatively safe. I say relatively safe because even though the limpet itself cannot graze it, a top shell or periwinkle will be happy to do so. It is quite common to find a periwinkle shell on top of a limpet shell busy grazing any settled seaweed spores. Isn't the rocky shore and its inhabitants a fascinating place!

Other creatures are soft bodied, but host a 'deadly' sting, to catch their prey. The anemones, hydroids and summer visiting jellyfish are stingers and catch their prey by stinging them. They in turn defend themselves from predators by emitting the sting. This allows such creatures to generally live openly, providing much beauty on the shore. So many more creatures float in and out and move too quickly to have their photo taken and so the research is ongoing. I do hope you will find enough lively detail in the following pages to keep you enthralled for a long time. Welcome to the wonderful animal world of the rocky shore.

Beadlet Anemone
(*Actinia equina*)

Both conspicuous and inconspicuous throughout the rocky shore, these simple creatures are aptly nick-named 'Flowers of the Sea' because of their colourful flower-like appearance. At Ross Beach, species living or visiting the shore include the most visible **Beadlet Anemone** (*Actinia equina*), the floppy tentacled **Snakelocks Anemone** (*Anemonia viridis*), the highly camouflaged and normally much smaller **Gem Anemone** (*Aulactinia verrucosa*), the sun-shy **Strawberry Anemone** (*Actinia fragracea*), the substantial, short tentacled **Daisy Anemone** (*Cereus pedunculatus*), the highly variable, lower shore pool living **Dahlia Anemone** (*Urticina felina*) and the cheerful Winter visitors, the **Elegant Anemone** (*Sagartia elegans*). Of this grouping the most common species are the Beadlet, Snakelocks and Gem anemones.

Together this group of sea creatures not only add colour and variety to the shore, but a sense of exotic sophistication not seen in other animals. For example comparing these creatures with the crabs on the shore, one senses the crab community might also appreciate the colourful beauty of these animals. Certainly, anemones appear to be less predated on than most other creatures, and while they release vicious stings to protect themselves, it is not evident, that much attack occurs beneath their stinging cells. Their main predators are starfish, cowries and nudibranch sea slugs, together with a few fish. As humans, fascination for these creatures has existed since Victorian times, when naturalists of the period attended outdoor classes for the study of marine natural history, similar to those offered through my Hedge School's Rocky Shore Explorations in the current day. Early illustrated books on these exotic creatures authored by Philip Henry Gosse and George Tugwell, were snapped up during this time.

Basic Structure of an Anemone.
Anemones are classed within the phylum Cnidaria – animals with stinging cells and they share this grouping with various other stinging creatures like hydroids and jellyfish. In the case of the anemone, its structure is made up of a cylindrical body called a column, at the bottom of which may be a basal disk that attaches the anemone to the substratum and allows it to move somewhat by muscular contractions. At the top of the column, is an oral disk, which contains a slit-like mouth to the centre. The mouth is surrounded by a grouping of hollow tentacles and the largest are those on the first row surrounding the mouth slit. From the mouth a flattened tube leads into the internal body of the anemone. This tube has grooves and hairs, which it uses to direct a flow of water into the body. This is used for respiration as well as controlling levels of water flow, which varies with inflation and deflation of the column. The internal body of the anemone is divided into six chambers, and each tentacle is directly connected to a chamber. These chambers contain the digestive, reproductive and muscular systems.

When out of water, most anemones can withdraw their tentacles and oral disk into the body cavity, for protection. To catch prey, anemones use a variety of stinging cells, which are triggered by sensory or chemical clues. These stinging cells can stun prey or sting predators. Touching a Beadlet anemone (*Actinia equina*), one feels a stickiness of their tentacles to ones fingers. This is the sting. In the case of the **Beadlet Anemone** (*Actinia equina*), the stinging cells are contained in circular bead-like warts at the top of the column, coloured blue. Beadlet Anemones sting other Beadlet Anemones from different families, if they come too close.
Anemones have not been known for their movement, preferring instead to sit and wait on prey. However my experiences on the shore, shows that there is alot more movement taking place amongst species than that suggested in textbooks.

Predatory behaviour.
Day to day living, the Anemone, waits for the waves to bring it food or for unsuspecting prey to wander too close to its stinging tentacles. I have observed **Snakelocks Anemones** attacking and gorging on rather large **Moon Jellyfish**, small crabs are known to be ingested whole with scraps of broken shell expelled later. Anemones positioning, especially that of the Beadlet Anemome, in maximum water flow of incoming tides assures them a rich variety of prey, and they can be major beneficiaries of disruptive wave action. Indeed they show no need to find shelter, when stone bashing strong waves plunder the shoreline, where they await their prey.

Beadlet Anemones

One of the few creatures on the rocky shore to live openly without the safety and shelter of a hard shell (mollusc), the **Beadlet Anemone**, can survive extremes of weather conditions and predators when out of water. It withdraws its tentacles(1), and sits motionless on the shore, often in colourful communities. It coats itself in a mucus membrane which prevents 'drying out' in hot sunshine conditions, and despite their colourful attractiveness, shore birds are not drawn to preying on them. Their highest density is distributed on the lower shore where they attach themselves to rock and boulder. This is a rich feeding ground with abundance of plankton, larvae, and small creatures floating inwards in the tide. As one reaches upper shore rockpools, their density is reduced to singular specimens living alone .

One of the highest living Anemones on the shore here at Ross, in a predominantly shell gravel pool with meagre pickings, this particular mature anemone, has positioned itself to make the most of its location aggressively waiting to snatch and sting the odd **Glass Prawn**, **Shrimp** or **Hermit Crab**, that comes within its grasp. Obviously, this horizontal location, on the corner of a rock has been strategically chosen for access to the greatest selection of prey. It is likely to have maintained this position for many years. Anemones are deemed to be ageless, and can live indefinitely - 500 years and more if the circumstances around it remain undisturbed. Thus this Anemone may be the oldest living creature in our area, a rocky shore generational linkage that may surpass our family's entire ten or more generations at Loophead! To the shore onlooker, It can look like a lonely life, though, as this singular Anemone has neither close family or friends! **Beadlet Anemones** are seen as 'sit and wait' predators.

Beadlet Anemone

Main body parts

1 - Column - main body.

2 - Blue Beadlet of Stinging Cells.

3 - Tentacles.

4 - Central Oral disk - Mouth.

Right: A golden coloured adult Beadlet with two juvenile green Beadlets. There is no parenting provided for the newly born.

Turning over a lower shore boulder, I am met with this beautiful palette of jelly like blobs. The colour variation of the Beadlet Anemone, brings a rich palette to the lower shore, if one is prepared to look for it. Under boulders like these, the young Beadlets are safe and secure from rough tides, dessication and potential prey. It is a great place to find juvenile Beadlets. It is interesting to note, that even though I have seen a significant number of baby light green Anemones, finding adults of this colour variant is not common. Young Beadlets are often nestled against an adult Beadlet, but in different colour combinations. It is common to see baby Anemones being cast out through the central oral disk of the Beadlet. This anemone reproduces viviparously meaning that instead of laying or producing eggs the mother simply produces direct babies.

Snakelocks Anemone

Snakelocks Anemone
Anemonia viridis

The long, plant like, colourful and straggly tentacles of the **Snakelocks Anemone**, are its defining feature. The colour can vary from the bright green form with purple tips to the uniform taupe variation. These Snakelocks are best seen in Summer, when they live attached to the **Sugar Kelp** and other seaweeds, close to the surface of the water, predominantly in the shallow sub-tidal. However, Sugar Kelp is an annual seaweed crop, normally detaching and landing onshore by late Autumn. Searching for Snakelocks in this debris biomass and not finding any, suggests that they have already moved location before the Kelp detaches.

During Winter months, one is most likely to encounter them attached to rock and boulder. Their distribution is not confined to the shallow-subtidal, and I have found them populating lower, middle and upper shore rockpools, in both exposed and sheltered positions. Unlike other anemones, the Snakelocks tentacles contain a symbiotic algae, and this is the main reasoning behind the quest for light for photosynthesis providing energy for itself and the Anemone. At Ross, during the warm Summer months, the abundant Snakelocks are a joy to behold as one wades through the waters of the sub-tidal. In Winter, they appear sparse.

When emersed, the majority of Snakelocks appear on the shore with a floppy mass of extended tentacles, however, it is possible for the snakelocks to fully withdraw their dense volume of chubby tentacles into their column when out of water as seen here. There are reports of stings from Snakelocks anemones causing rash and other effects that take time to heal.

Above: This relaxing Snakelocks is undisturbed by my presence. Its response system seems much slower than that of the crabs for instance.

The Snakelocks Anemone can reproduce by longitudinal fission, a means by which they just tear off part of their body to create a new individual and an exact clone of its parent. When viewing a grouping of Snaklocks living close together like the left image, it is most likely that they reproduced using the method described here.

Snakelocks Anemone

Detaching Basal Disk

The distribution of the Snakelocks Anemone in British & Irish Waters is confined to the Southern and Western Coasts reaching north to the Scottish Isles.

This light coloured Snakelocks (1) is well camouflaged amongst a dense growth and diversity of seaweed in a middle shore pool. Here its sticky thread-like sting will catch plankton, larvae, small fish and crustaceans.

Light coloured variations of this anemone are much less frequently encountered on the shore here.

Gem/Wartlet Anemone

Gem Anemone
Aulactinia verrucosa

The generally smaller size and cryptic coloration of the **Gem Anemone**, whereby it survives in the midst of crustose Coralline algae, and mottled sands, meant that it took sharp observation to actually see any on the shore, and when found, they almost always had partially or fully withdrawn tentacles. Indeed it was only late Summer 2013 when I eventually found a photo opportunity that yielded the above image of a fully extended individual occupying an upper shore pool, a rare location, in an assemblage with pebbles, broken shell and mineral rock. Coming face to face with such exquisite beauty was visually exhilarating!

Initially, I had let myself believe that in not seeing them very often, that these highly camouflaged creatures were quite rare here.. How wrong I was!

The Gem Anemone can often be found under a layer of gravel/sand in the shallow sub-tidal or in rockpools in the same conditions as well as under seaweeds on the lower shore often in close proximity to Coralline algae.

Gem Anemones with babies

The shiny wet surfaces combined with the rich bio-diverse vegetative and animal settlement on sheltered lower shore rocks, causes one to slow down and examine carefully, the immense detail of every small segment. At least twenty **Gem Anemones** including their now transparent young are settled within this image together with a range of crustose and foliose algae of the red, brown and green varieties. Given my encounters with un-parented young on the lower shore during March/April (see page 96), it appears that there is more than one process of reproduction taking place.   A site played out time and again on the lower shore at Ross. These pink wart-like columns range to 5cm in diameter. Mostly found on the Western and Southern coasts of Britain & Ireland, their northern limit.

Strawberry Anemone

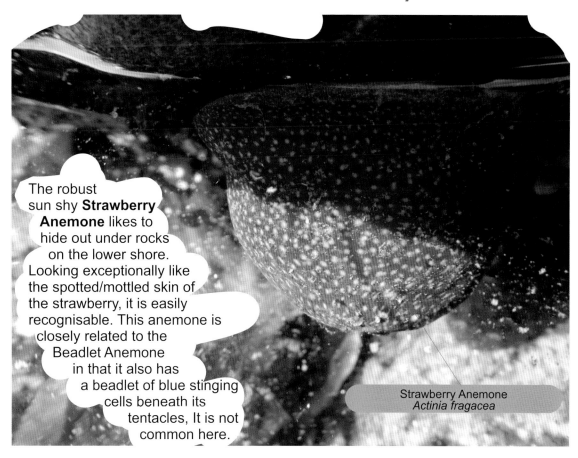

The robust sun shy **Strawberry Anemone** likes to hide out under rocks on the lower shore. Looking exceptionally like the spotted/mottled skin of the strawberry, it is easily recognisable. This anemone is closely related to the Beadlet Anemone in that it also has a beadlet of blue stinging cells beneath its tentacles, It is not common here.

Strawberry Anemone
Actinia fragacea

Daisy Anemone

Daisy Anemone
Cereus pedunculatus

Unlike the Strawberry Anemone, this **Daisy Anemone** which resides in an upper shore pool, plays a cryptic game, and was barely visible amongst the dead shell sediment. It's disk size of approx 10cm together with its large quantity of mottled tentacles (normally 500-1000)were visible, whilst its column was buried beneath the gravel. When I moved to touch, it rapidly hid its entire self beneath the gravel. Found all around the Irish Coast.

Dahlia Anemone

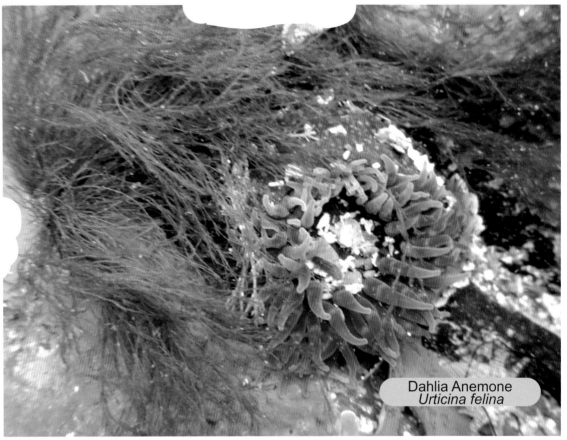

Dahlia Anemone
Urticina felina

In the depths of a lower shore rock pool, beneath wrack coverage, the **Dahlia Anemone** prefers such hidden away anonymity. Here it is surrounded by **Common Green Branched Weed** and **Crustose Coralline algae**.

Dahlia Anemone

The **Dahlia Anemone** is capable of ingesting whole juvenile crabs among other prey.

It's a sheer delight to encounter one of the beautifully coloured Dahlia Anemones, and at Ross, the prime spotting location is at the bottom of deep rock pools on the lower shore, tucked away from the limelight amongst the seaweed. They may also be encountered in the shallow subtidal coated over in broken shell fragments. I have also encountered them reproducing by a process of longitudinal fission - separating into two anemones from one. This is interesting.

Distinctive banding on the 160 or so tentacles is amongst their features although uniform coloured individuals may also occur. Quite a large anemone to 15cm diameter and found around the Western & Southern Irish Coast.

Dahlia Anemone

Dahlia Anemone

Strolling along the shallow sub-tidal at low Spring Tide, and the Dahlia Anemone has found a way to camouflage and protect itself when in shallow waters, exposed to birds, humans and anemone-eating nudibranch sea slugs. This may also be its own predatory strategy. It coats itself (by mucus adhesion) in locally found shell particles and sediment, withdraws its tentacles and as a result I nearly missed it. This 'flexible shell' is a protection mechanism from been gorged on by the free floating Nudibranch Sea Slugs and Cowries. In this way its behaviour differs immensely from that of the Beadlet Anemone, who appears to have no fear of being fully exposed out of water, living much closer to the inner shore where the Nudibranch sea slugs rarely wander.

Elegant Anemone

Elegant Anemone
Sagartia elegans

We first encountered the **Elegant Anemone** in middle shore rock pools during late December 2009. We noted their disappearance by mid - March 2010. During our continuous research of the beach over each of the subsequent years, we have noted an interesting migratory pattern emerging: Late December an entourage of up to one hundred Elegant Anemones, big and small arrive/ are tossed into the same combination of middle shore pools. Just a few available pools. They will nestle close to the upper verges half hidden by Carrigeen, and they will also occupy more exposed positions on the floor of the pool. Pool depths vary, and the anemones are highly conspicuous because of their sunny colouration. They appear to depart in batches, with all individuals departed by mid-April. March 2014 has arrived and I believe I have finally found a 'logical' purpose for their visitation...

Elegant Anemone

Possible Migratory Pattern

In transit

Amid the bounty, diversity and sheer size of sub-tidal seaweeds, a lone **Elegant/Sandalled/White-striped Anemone** balled up and in transit. Both species are normally sub-tidal species living on rocky substrata to 50m depths. Also in the picture the red **Discoid Fork Weed** (*Polyides rotundus*), **Sugar Kelp** (*Saccharina latissima*), **Carrigeen Moss** (*Chondrus crispus*) and an unidentified filamentous brown seaweed.

Of importance in identifying the **Elegant Anemone**, are the white warty looking spots on the outside of its column. For a period of time we had mistaken this species for the Sandalled/White-striped Anemone (*Actinothoe sphyrodeta*) because of its similiar colouring. However the Sandalled Anemone has a distinctive stripe effect on the outside of its column.

The Elegant Anemone has up to 120 pointed tentacles. There is also a rose pink variety of this species.

The Seasearch Distribution Map (2010) shows a distribution of this anemone along the Southern and Western coast of Ireland.

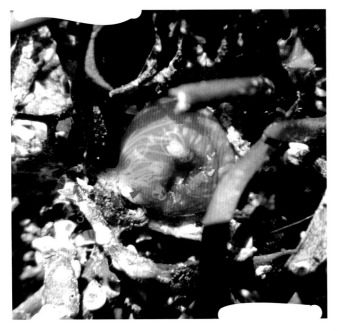

Elegant Anemone
Development on the Shore

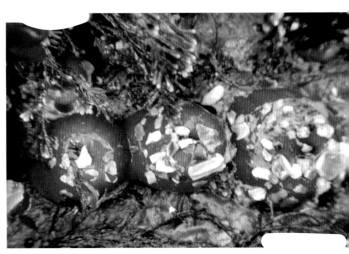

Here on the fringe of the North East Atlantic Ocean at Ross Beach, on the final edge of March, nestled amongst the holdfasts and stipes of the small red Carrígeen seaweed, now looking relatively large, I zoom in on the tiny orange blobs. Having been here in early March, when I first photographed them (1), they each measured approx 5-6mm and were unformed polyps attached to this substratum and shaded by the Carrígeen's fronds. On the same rock, on the same day I found the predator Nudibranch sea slug of the same bright hues. Two weeks later, and the above images (2),(3) and (4) unfold. Visibly developing Elegant Anemones *(Sagartia elegans)*, complete with gullet, developing tentacles, and external warty structures. At last a 'logical' answer to the inward pool migration that lasted from December to March. My 'logical' conclusion is that it is to aid the 'fertilization' process. Within the confines of a small pool, fertilization is bound to be more successful. Of course, it may be due to they being simply tossed ashore by the ocean into the same pools each December, or a heretofore unestablished linkage with Carrigeen, or some other 'illogical' reason. These anemones are not confined to just one process of reproduction with 'basal reproduction' generating a 'cloned community' being another form of reproduction.

Summer Visitors - Jelly-like Hydroids
(*Aequorea vitrina*)

The jelly-like Hydroid *Aequorea vitrina* does not appear to have a common name. As a Hydroid and not a Jelly, it consists of a colony of small individuals instead of one singular specimen. It can appear saucer-like or umbrella like, and has a 'crystal' clear solid jelly mass. This creature has a two phase life-cycle, the first being as a polyp attached to rock. In the Spring it grows and develops into a pelagic Hydroid as seen here, spending approx six months at sea before dying off in the Autumn.

I am grateful for expert assistance with the identification of this creature from the Seasearch Identifications community on Facebook. Members were able to advise that they are common in Norwegian waters and have been common around Orkney during the past two years.

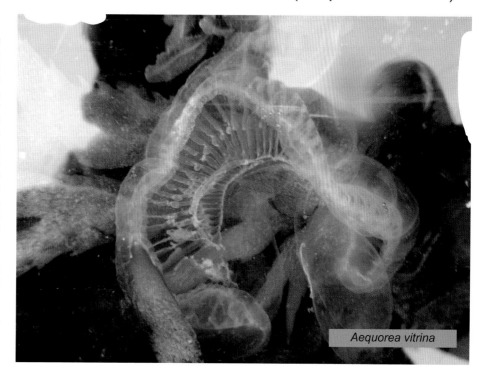

Aequorea vitrina

Right - This is an image of the same species taken in late April 2013. Note the crystal, glass-like transparency of this little creature which measures approx 10cms in diameter. I found it alone in a shallow lower shore pool. These are bio-luminescent creatures, who can light up in the dark.

This family grouping has a very significant research history. Research of **Aequorea** spp. by three scientists Drs. Osamu Shimomura, Martin Chalfie and Roger Tsien, whereby they discovered the luminescent protein aequorin and the flourescent molecule GFP (Green Flourescent Protein), led to they being awarded the Nobel Peace Prize in Chemistry in 2008.

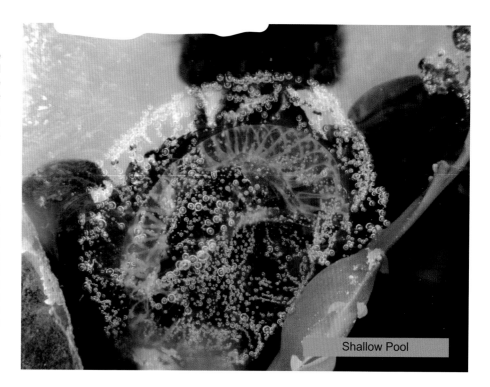

Shallow Pool

Summer Visitors - Jellies

Moon Jellyfish
(*Aurelia aurita*)

The **Moon Jellyfish** (*Aurelia aurita*), is generally a pelagic ocean drifter, living entirely in the ocean. One magical characteristic of these creatures is their ability to produce light i.e bio-luminesence. Lighting up in the dark in the deep ocean, bio-luminescence is used predominantly as a form of communication between animals, and can be used for defense, offense, and intraspecific communication. Many animals use bio-luminescence in multiple ways, though jellyfish use it primarily for defense. It is important to note, however, that the different ways in which jellyfish use bio-luminescence are still being discovered.

The Moon Jellyfish, is a stinging jelly closely related to Anemones. Anemones prey on Jellyfish and win. They tend to come inshore in swarms during warm weather in the late Summer months. During the warm Summer of 2013, hundreds of juveniles also descended on the shore at Ross approx 2cms diameter. The first stage of the Moon Jelly's life cycle is that of a sessile polyp attached to substratum.

A less common visitor to our shore at Ross is another pelagic Jellyfish, the **Blue Jellyfish** (*Cyanea lamarckii*). I first discovered a small number of these much bigger and exotic looking jellies during the warm summer of 2013. They would float in with one tide, stay on the shore and then float out to sea again. They didn't appear to enjoy rainy days on the shore. They normally appeared, blue side up. However on turning one over on the shore, one finds masses of browny cream tentacles, not a pretty site, when out of water. There are differing opinions as to the strength of its sting, my advice would be to not touch it directly.

Blue Jellyfish
(*Cyanea lamarckii*)

The Blue Jellyfish, sometimes known as the Bluefire Jellyfish is also bio-luminescent and can look astonishingly beautiful in this mode. My research however is confined to the onshore in daylight and I have to depend on the images of others to remark this special characteristic.

Black Sea Cucumber
(Holothuria forskali)

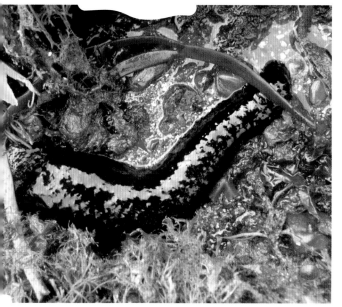

Black Sea Cucumber washed up

Black Sea Cucumber - Shallow Sub-tidal

The rocky shore environment can be defined by a series of sub-habitats as well as zones. Certain organisms are very particular to their location and, narrowly defined habitat. The large worm like **Black Sea Cucumber – Cotton Spinner** seen above, occupies a benthic location on the shallow sub-tidal, where it colonises on soft gravel sediment. At Ross, this is a specific defined location on the beach and hence the Black Sea Cucumber may generally be located only at this location. However, they are sometimes seen landed on the beach and in rockpools due to rough seas. The colony does not appear too large numbering around twenty individuals. This creature burrows into the sandy sediment and can be well covered over by Kelp fronds, so my number may be underestimated.

The Black Sea Cucumber is often seen motionless in the Summer waters, where, its cryptic positioning amongst a myriad of seaweeds and gravel, may cause it to be easily overlooked. At best, slow moving, it can crawl on short feet or by using the muscular wall of its body. This creature has a life span of five to ten years, and feeds on plankton and organic sediments. It has mucus covered tentacles to assist in capturing its prey. The cucumber is preyed on by starfish, crabs and in other parts of the world, humans. When threatened it releases a toxin Holothurin in white sticky threads. When frightened, it can eject its entire intestines. Experiencing this at first hand, before we got to know the Sea Cucumber well, we felt just as frightened as the Cucumber did. It can regenerate new intestines.

Of most interest is the fact that the Sea Cucumber, is highly sought after in Asian countries as a food and flavouring source and as a result are actually over fished in many locations. The Sea cucumber is boiled and its intestines are expelled, its body shortens and thickens and these dried delicacies are traded in countries like Hong Kong, Japan, Taiwan and the Galapagos Isles.

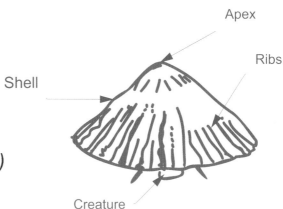

Apex

Ribs

Shell

Creature

Limpets *(Patella spp.)*

One of the most visible and common fauna on the North East Atlantic rocky shore, the Common Limpet *(Patella vulgata),* locally known as Bárnach, settle throughout the shore, from the fringes of the shallow sub-tidal to the upper shore, their distribution greatly decreasing at the upper limit. Here their semi - permanent home is a particular spot (home scar) on the rock, a place to which they return after each grazing foray, a rugged or smooth spot to which their shell formation has adopted to fit smugly. We have pictorially monitored this phenomenon over the past couple of years, and it is incredible the accuracy with which they return to their little spot on the rock, even if wedged between a whole settlement.

Walking along the shore, seeing so many Limpets 'fastened to rock' one may get the impression that limpets are non-movers. However, during periods of tidal submersion on the lower shore, Limpets can be seen to move slowly, their shell lifted less than 5mm off the substratum, while they graze what looks like bare rock. With a sharp tooth like structure, called a radula, Limpets are keen grazers of bio-film, diatoms, sporlings of macro algae and cyanobacteria, that are abundant, if not seen by the naked eye on this 'bare' rock. The lower shore in particular provides ample grazing grounds as new settlements arrive with each tide. Limpets on the middle shore are more inclined to feed during night time, while emersed. This strategy is used to prevent predation by shore birds.

As one ascends the rocky shore vertically, *Patella vulgata*, can be encountered, on open rock, underneath overhangs, in rock crevices, at the bottom of rockpools, amongst the barnacles in the barnacle zone, and occasionally on the extreme upper shore. It is thought that Limpets ascend vertically over time, and certainly the few that we have encountered at the upper limit, appear to have attained great age - judging by size and wear and tear of shell, and lichen growth on shell.

Of course, those who migrate up-shore to its higher limits, have to endure greater threats to survival. There is the possibility of dessication, during the hot Summer Months, with little moisture, and little food either reaching, or surviving on hot, dry rock. There is a greater threat from shore birds like oystercatchers, gulls and crows, as the Limpets are exposed for long periods of time out of water. In winter there is the threat of icy conditions, whereby the moving, grazing Limpet will be unable to use its muscular foot to cling tight and clamp down at rapid notice.

Limpets have both inter-tidal and terrestrial predators. Inter-tidal predators include starfish, crabs and dog whelks. Terrestrial predators include various coastal birds. Limpets are fighters and to stave off attacks from starfish and dog whelks for example, they use a combination of stomping and mushrooming, swinging their shell to off load dog-whelks or rapid stomping of their razor edged shell on the arms of the starfish predator.

Limpets

Common Limpet
Patella vulgata

A limpet community living on sandstone on the lower
shore at Ross. Note the variety of positions held.

Limpets - a traditional seafood.

No discussion on the Limpet could be complete without documenting the important role that it played in the dietary requirements of local coastal communities. The limpet was a popular coastal food, especially on Fridays, but when the Great Irish Famine hit (1845 -1852) the Limpet was a critical source of protein and essential minerals and vitamins. Limpets greatly helped sustain local coastal communities around Ireland.

My parents with their long ancestral linkages to Loophead, relay the story that the Limpets became extinct at Ross Beach during this period because of the huge dependency on them, even if the beach was owned and patrolled by the landlord of the era. Ross Beach was an easily accessible beach, with no significant vertical cliffs and the limpets were within easy reach.

Subsequent to the famine, many people turned away from the shore, associating it with the famine and extreme poverty. Being adjacent to the beach however, our family upheld the tradition of foraging for Bárnachs (Limpets) especially on Fridays. We were sent to the beach with tin cans and had to beat the Limpets off the rock with rock after school. We collected seawater and they were boiled in this for approx 15 minutes. There was mixed feelings as to the tastiness of this rather rubbery delicacy. I have not foraged for Limpets, (now preferring to observe them), since the 1970s but I think it might be a better idea to boil the sea water then blanche the limpets in the boiling water, perhaps a more tenderized dish awaits!

Limpets - and Elements

Adult Limpet size and shell vary quite significantly depending on their location on the shore. James, has been conducting an exacting survey of this theory. Encountering a Common Limpet settlement in the Barnacle Zone, on a rugged rock combination of sandstone, mudstone and shale, mostly to the eastern side of the direct tidal surge, it becomes apparent that the general size of these limpets is relatively small, with average size of 2.5 -3 cm long. The shells are highly ribbed often with orange ribbing, which is possibly due to the abundance of iron oxide close to the rock surface. On other parts of the middle shore, on formations to the east of the tidal surge at Ross, Limpet settlements lead a sheltered life occupying crevices and under hangs, and the result of this shelter is evident in their shell with pointed apexes and radial ribbing fully intact. Lower shore settlements in the direct tidal surge have smooth or dis-configured shell and rounded apexes.

During the Summer of 2013, I had a group of Hawaiian tourists on one of my rocky shore exploration field trips. They were aghast on sight of the significant population of the Limpets on the shore. They were in fact brimming with excitement on viewing them. In Hawaii, their Limpet species is known as **Opihi**, a very traditional delicacy, so difficult to obtain now due to severe over harvesting, that the prices fetched for small but legal sizes is exorbitant and the quantities available for harvesting have decreased from 140,000tonnes to just 13,000tonnes per annum..

Common Limpet

A lower shore settlement of *Patella vulgata* - on the *sheltered side* of exposed rock, hence not in full exposure of the tidal surge.

1 Sheltering Limpets - middle shore - note apexes pointed and ribs intact.

2 Exposed Limpets - Lower shore this community may be that of the China Limpet *(Patella aspera)* whose apex is generally anterior. It is the same story though, as their ribs have been worn and their apex rounded.

Limpet observations

1

An Algae 'Brown Limpet Paint' *(Ralfsia verrucosa)* atop Limpet. This is common on Limpet shells from the lower to the lower middle shore.

2

Limpet 'Home Scar' The Common Limpet lives on the same spot - a home to which he returns to after each grazing foray. As a result, this scar becomes visible on the shore, often abraded, and more so with the ageing of the Common Limpet.

3

Green Algae *Ulva spp.* atop Limpet. Limpets have to contend with carrying all sorts of growth and creatures on their back. This is particularly evident amongst lower shore individuals.

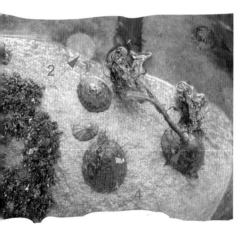

4

A well established Bladder Wrack *(Fucus vesiculosus)* atop limpet on lower shore making movement in rocky areas difficult.

6

In January, a juvenile Limpet, measuring approx 6mm settled in a tiny groove on open rock surface. It will have to move position as it attains growth, as this groove is too small for full development. It is also worthy to note its capability of surviving severe winter storms unparented.

5

A lower shore Limpet clad in bio-mass and foliose *Ulva spp.* on a grazing mission.

1 The Common Dog Whelk *(Nucella lapillus)* attacking a Common Limpet *(Patella vulgata)* The Dog Whelk will use its radula to grind at the shell, whilst when the Limpet realises it is being attacked *(probably through vibration/sound),* it will lift its shell high and swirl to knock off the Dog Whelk. This is known as mushrooming.

2 At the bottom of a Coralline spp. (2a) encrusted lower shore rockpool, the Limpet too has become covered in a pink Coralline coating. Limpets do not tend to graze on hardened calcified algae, but rather the bio-film over it.

3 At the very top of the upper zone of Ross Beach, a rare site of a well matured Limpet surviving a much more challenging environment than its lower/middle shore comrades. Limpets may live up to 20 years.

4 At the bottom of a Coralline spp. (2a) encrusted lower shore rockpool, this Limpet has not been over grown with the algae, perhaps a new resettler

5 Clearly visible Limpet grazing/mucus trails, these in turn attract new settlements of bio-film ensuring a continuous supply of food.

Limpet shadows

Casting tall shadows in the Winter sun, some lower shore Limpets, cast a circular shell shape and low vertical profile, perhaps yielding a stronger holding on the heavily washed smooth sandstone

Two-headed Wrack

All dressed up on the middle shore, this heavily ribbed limpet is sporting the rarely encountered **Two-headed Wrack** (*Fucus distichus*) on top. In this position the Two-headed Wrack is secure from the grazing activity of the gastropod. If its sporeling had settled on the rock surface nearby, it would more than likely not have survived the limpets grazing.

Blue-rayed Limpet
(Helicon pellucidum)

Blue-rayed Limpet
(Helicon pellucidum)

Eventually, finding these most attractive Blue-rayed Limpets in the shallow sub-tidal in late Winter, where there were up to 20 of them big and small lined up on a long piece of Kelp, the Blue-rayed Limpet is not a 'true' Limpet. It was after storm Catherine, after their normal habitat, the Kelp Forest in the shallow sub-tidal had been particularly badly decimated. This short living mollusc (normal life time - less than one year) buries itself into the fronds of the kelp providing a safe sanctuary in exposed conditions. Kelps however, often suffer the greatest losses when rough ocean storms hit the shore. This little creature has a thin shell, with blue light rays. These rays are due to diffraction of light by the reflection caused by bending around the shell. This diffraction is common to all molluscan shells but is dependent on the groove density and the surface quality of the shell and is therefore not always visible. This is an issue of physics and goes well beyond the scope of this book.

Green Sea Urchin & Rock-boring Urchin

(Psammechinus miliaris) & (Paracentrotus lividus)

Rock-boring Urchin

One of natures, prettiest, creatures related to Starfish because of their spiny skins and symmetrical shapes, the rich colours and rock burrowing abilities of the **Rock-boring Urchin** (*Paracentrotus lividus*) are fascinating. These are grazers who graze on the tough calcareous encrusting seaweeds and scrape themselves into a home on the rock. I have just encountered a few of these in a singular spectacular pool on the extreme lower shore. They are generally a warm water species.

Further down on the shore, at Ross Beach, I encountered a singular **Green Sea Urchin** (*Psammechinus miliaris*) hidden beneath a boulder. This specie is much smaller and has a colouring akin to that of the Snakelocks Anemone. I haven't encountered them very often here, but I believe they can be more common a little further up the coast.

Barnacles *(Chthamalus sp.)*

Barnacles, perhaps the most abundant species on the Rocky shore...

Barnacles are tiny crustaceans that are affixed to rock by a calcified cement. They generally have an off-white/grey tri-angular shape with six plates at the top, which open and close to draw in food and perform reproduction function. They occupy a very distinctive vertical band on the rocky shore which is often referred to as the Barnacle Zone. This band stretches to the top of the middle shore. Within this zone, there are areas of tightly packed settlements of the kite-shaped openings of the **Barnacle** *(Chthamalus sp.)*, the only species I have discovered here at Ross. Barnacles remain attached to the same rock for their entire life. They are 'suspension feeders' which means that when the tide comes in over them, they open up the six plates on top, and their hairy legs (cirri) grab tiny particles of plankton that is abundant and floating in the water. When the tide goes out, the plates firmly close again. Much of our current knowledge about barnacles is based on the work of eminent biologist Charles Darwin, who dedicated eight years (1846-1854) to studying them. It is likely that this extensive study of barnacles had a significant influence on the development of Darwin's seminal theory of natural selection that he published in 1859.

Dense Barnacle Settlement

A dense settlement of Barnacles on middle shore rock. The Limpets in the image do not attack the Barnacles. Also in the picture a juvenile **Common Whelk (***Buccinum undatum***)**

The **Goose Barnacle** (*Lepas anatifera*) is an entirely pelagic member of the Barnacle Family. It attaches itself to all sorts of ocean debris and has only ever made a temporary tidal visit to Ross Beach.

Lurking and sheltering amongst the dense settlements of Barnacles the **Small Periwinkle** (*Littorina neritoides*) is often found in small numbers within predated Barnacle shells.

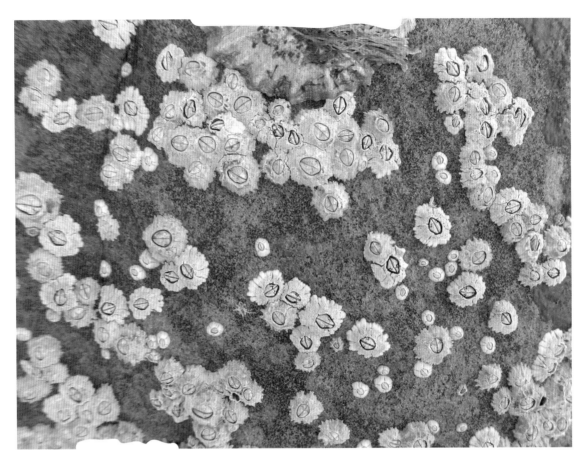

Above : The predated Barnacle shell becomes a valuable shelter for the juvenile **Rough Periwinkle** (*Littorina saxatalis*).

Sometimes the settlement of Barnacles is so tightly packed, many individuals are forced to develop a tall columnar shape. This weakens the Barnacles grip on rock with a smaller base, storm tides can easily knock them off. Perhaps the reasoning behind their tight settlement can be explained in terms of their reproduction process. Each Barnacle is a hermaphrodite with both male and female organs. The Barnacle will fertilize neighbouring individuals by means of an extensible penis, and so the Barnacles being fertilized need to be relatively close by. Where individual or loosely colonized settlements appear on rock, they will be more than likely sterile, even though it is thought that Barnacles can self fertilize. Fertilized larvae is expelled into the ocean during the months of March/April. Here the pelagic larvae morphs into a number of larval phases surviving for at least a couple of weeks before carefully selecting a settling position on rocky substrata. It can identify its own species, and will set itself on rock adjacent to an adult community. At this point it cements itself and metamorphizes into the barnacle form as we know it within 24 hours. *The above photo was taken during the month of June, when the young Barnacles have grown into a visible size but are still not fully grown adults. Barnacles typically live for three to five years.*

Common Dog Whelk
(Nucella lapillus)

Nucella lapillus
Common Dog whelk

The carnivore - Common Dog Whelk *(Nucella lapillus)* - is a major feature on the Barnacle Zone on the Beach, where this slow moving gastropod can be seen attached to its prey for long periods of time.

Female Dog Whelk laying eggs

The **Comon Dog Whelk** begins its life in the fertilized egg capsule laid by the female throughout the year – most especially in Autumn and Spring. The above photo was taken in late January. The image was taken from an overturned rock, from the lower shore and is also festooned with calcareous Tube Worms, Porcelain Crabs, Sea Fir hydroid, ascidians and other creatures. This suggests a treacherous environment full of likely predators. The eggs have been fertilized before leaving the female, during a copulation process, where the whelks aggregate on the shore. Although, each capsule contains hundreds of eggs, only few are fertile, and the rest provide food for the developing gastropod, which will bite its way free from the capsule after an approx period of four months. This is known as direct recruitment. By this time the parent has left the scene, and the young whelk is left to fend for itself.

Our survey of the dead shell gravel on the shore at Ross, showed up more young Common Dog Whelk shell fully intact than any other. This may suggest that the young Whelk has a relatively high mortality rate, or it may also suggest the relative strength of its hard shell. Whelks have an approx life span of seven years.

As a predator, the young whelk will have to prey on the young of barnacles, mussels and limpets to survive. Once settled on a particular diet, the Dog Whelk does not change its diet. The fully grown whelk, has a thick , strong shell, which helps it to survive the onslaught of crabs and birds. It has been found that the shell of the Common Dog Whelk, living on sheltered shores is much thicker with a narrower aperture than that of those at an exposed location with strong currents. It is believed that this is direct response to its environment, where it is more prone to attack on a sheltered shore.

extendable radula

predator with prey

The dog Whelk, armed with its thick shell is extremely slow moving, and on choosing a suitably sized prey to attack, (at Ross, mostly barnacles), it will take up to 48 hours to extract the prey. The whelk firstly prizes open the plates of the barnacle, then injects an enzyme that liquidizes the flesh of the barnacle and it then sucks it out. The whelks will normally be found in the Barnacle Zone from the middle shore down to the lower shore, and can hide in crevices without food during turbulent periods for several days.

The Common Dog Whelk is distributed on both sides of the North Atlantic.

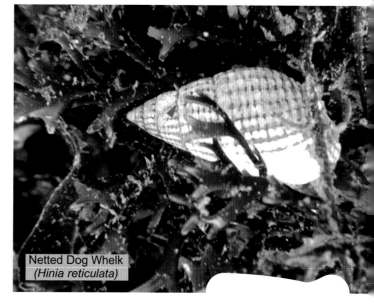
Netted Dog Whelk
(Hinia reticulata)

The Netted Dog Whelk, *(Hinia reticulata)* has a different appearance, habitat and diet. With a strong 'netted' sculptural shell, I have located them much lower down the shore in the shallow sub-tidal zone, apparently they survive to 50m sub-littoral. Their main diet is dead and decaying animal matter and they have a good sense of smell for this. The Netted Dog Whelk is native to the North East Atlantic. In late Spring I have located tiny juveniles measuring approx 1mm, with fully developed netted shell structures.

Rockpool Assemblage

Upper Shore

A colourful assemblage of the living and the dead in a rockpool on the upper shore at Ross. Amongst the shell collection, a single **Cowrie** *(Trivia monacha)*, **Topshells** *(Gibbula umbilicalis)* & *(Calliostoma zizyphinum)*, **Common Limpe**t *(Patella vulgata)*, and especially **Musse**l *(Mytilus edulis)*. Amongst the living; **Glass Prawn** *(Palaemon elegans)* and **Edible Periwinkle** *(Littorina littorea)*. It is worthy to note that most, if not all the dead shells have been washed into this pool and did not die in situ, as species like the Cowrie and Mussel are out of range of their normal habitat.

Common Mussel
(Mytilus edulis)

Mussel bed in rock crevice

Living 18-24 years, the Common Mussel is a bivalve suspension feeding scavenger

At Ross, it would be correct to state that the Common Mussel beds found in the intertidal zone are both small and sheltered away. Mostly found in surge channels, and wedged in rock crevices, it is fair to say that the mussel beds are quite insignificant in terms of size with just a couple hundred individuals present. Walking the gravel shore and analysing the gravel sediment throughout the shore, it becomes apparent, that significant quantities of the Common Mussel are to be found, perhaps sub-tidally in the bay region or exposed outer shore rock formations. I am grateful, therefore for the small colonies on the shore, as it provides me with fodder for study. In general, these wild mussels are small approx 3-4cm long by 1-2 cm wide.

Mussels are sessile filter suspension feeders, opening their bivalve shells when submerged in water, filtering particles of plankton and diatoms and algae sporelings together with biological deitritus. As such they are viewed as scavengers, for the range of food they are willing to ingest. Being sessile, they remain attached in position by means of a strong brown byssus thread to rocky substrata for their entire lives. Their lifespan can stretch from 18-24 years. They can survive in freezing conditions for several months, and have a Northern Arctic distribution together with distribution on both sides of the North Atlantic. Survival is precarious, with avian and shore predators, including the aforementioned dog whelk, herring gulls, crows, crabs and common starfish. Mussels will most likely be attacked when they open their bivalves to breathe or take in food particles.

Common Mussel
(Mytilus edulis)

Common Mussel - *Mytilus edulis* has both male and female individuals, the female being the larger. Spawning takes place between April and September and is dependent on environmental factors such as temperature and currents. Both sexes release gametes which are fertilized externally. The larvae, metamorphoses normally over a period of 20 -30 days, and mortality rates from settlements in exposed shores can be as high as 98%.

Coat of Mail Chiton
(Lepidochitona cinerea)

Coat of Mail Chiton
(Lepidochitona cinerea)

It may be difficult to locate the Coat of Mail Chiton on the rocky shore because of its cryptic colouration. Indeed textbooks associate this little mollusc mainly with the lower shore and shallow sub-tidal. My experience has been that of encountering them on upper shore rockpools beneath pool rocks, often in the company of young topshells and periwinkles. Like the limpet in many respects, it lives attached to rock, by way of a muscular foot and grazes on micro algae which it scrapes off the rock with its strong teeth attached to its tongue. It's defining feature are the eight interlocking plates, which allow it to roll into a ball if disturbed. Seen above with Carrigeen (*Chondrus crispus*) and the Purple Topshell (*Gibbula umbilicalis*)

Painted Topshell
(Calliostoma zizyphinum)

(1)Pointed Apex

(2)Fleshy salmon coloured animal

Upper Shore Pool

Where the dead shell remains in a decorative assemblageat the bottom of an upper shore rock pool, having washed up to this higher level, waiting for a Hermit Crab!.

Long since admired, this is one of the most attractive gastropods, because of its attractive spiral, pointed cone shell which measures up to 3cm tall by 3cm wide. I used to only encounter its dead shell. This grazing gastropod mollusc actually lives way down in the lower shore/shallow sub-tidal, grazing on rocks and boulders that are heavily clad in micro and macro algae. At Ross, there are numerous individuals to be found at this level, and it is normally found singularly. During ocean turbulence, it will seek shelter in crevices and under rock. It can be found sub-tidally to 300m. The female spawns a line of eggs, that are then fertilized by the male that hatch out on the shore into baby molluscs. It is distributed along the East Atlantic and the Mediterrean Sea.

Toothed Topshell
Osilinus lineatus

Grey Topshell
Gibbula cineraria

Flat Topshell
Gibbula umbilicalis

The **Toothed Topshell** (*Osilinus lineatus*) seen here grazing at the bottom of an upper shore rock pool at Ross, is in fact a Southern species of topshell, originating in the Mediterranean. Much study has been done to seek a correlation between its upward distribution to parts of the British Isles and that of increasing ocean temperatures. I do have memories going back to the 1970s of seeing this Topshell at Ross Beach. The Toothed Topshell can live to fifteen years, and it keeps growing to the end, (except during Winter months), its age can be measured by growth lines in its bulky rounded shell, which is much more rounded than that of the Edible Periwinkle. One of four Topshells found at Ross, this specie lives at the highest levels on the beach on bare rock and boulder. It tolerates full sun, and it avoids dessication by virtue of shutting its operculum (a circular disk that plugs entry to the animal inside). The female releases eggs which are fertilized externally during the Summer, and a young snail is formed from the larvae stage after 6 weeks, settling on boulder at an approx size of 1mm, but should have reached 6mm by Winter. The Toothed Topshell grazes on micro-algae.

The **Grey Topshell** (*Gibbula cineraria*) occupies a completely different habitat than the much larger Toothed Topshell. The Grey Topshell, lives low down on the shore and in the sub-tidal to 130m. Here, in this wet environment, it grazes on micro and macro algae. It is known to have a diurnal migration pattern, whereby the topshell moves up to the top of rocks during the daytime and retreat down shore in the darkness and independent of the tides. It is a bluntly conical topshell. A distinctive feature of all topshells is the 'mother of pearl' coating on the inside of the shell. With sand and other abrasives, wearing the outer shell over time, the 'mother of pearl' may be seen on the outside of the shell, towards its top. This topshell is common all around the British Isles, with varying shades of colour, some being darker, and all have a blotchy pattern.

Topshells

The **Purple/Flat topshell** (*Gibbula umbilicalis*) is the smallest member of the Topshell family, found around our coast. A most attractive shell with purple patterning against a light grey background, I have found it on all levels of the shore, grazing in a range of habitats, from the Serrated Wrack (*Fucus serratus*) of the lower shore to under rocks on shallow upper shore pools. In this latter habitat, it is worthy to note that this particular grazing aggregation generally look juvenile, much smaller in size than elsewhere. Safe and warmer at the end of Summer, it is possible that juvenile topshells, like crabs seek a particular, safe haven in which to grow and develop, safely away from most predators. Studies have shown that this particular topshell prefers a flatter, sheltered rocky shore with bound boulder, making Ross beach a perfect habitat.

Rockpool (under boulder) Assemblage - Upper Shore

Winter Assemblage

Winter (December) Assemblage - beneath rock in an upper shore rockpool - above the Barnacle Zone. A wonderful diversity in a small select and (safe) habitat consisting of **Purple/Flat Topshell** (*Gibbula umbilicalis*), **Grey Topshell** (*Gibbula cineraria*), **Edible Periwinkle** (*Littorina littorea*), **Beadlet Anemone** (*Actinia equina*), **Green Starlet** (*Asterina phylactia,*) **Sponge**, (*possibly Hymeniacidon perleve*), **Coiled Tube Worm** (*Spirobis* spp.) and algae. All available space on the rock is covered in a visible and non-visible biofilm. Competition between species for the available food supply exists and all mobile species were concentrated in the corner of the rock as shown. The exceptional winter storm Catherine accompanied by the highest tides in decades during January 2013, may have seen the demise of this assemblage, as rocks were hurled throughout the beach, ending up at locations out of habitat, carrying with them their assemblages like that shown above.

Edible Periwinkle

(Littorina littorea)

Edible periwinkle grazing in a middle shore rockpool on a range of micro algae.

The **Edible Periwinkle** (*Littorina littorea*) is one of the most recognised gastropods of the rocky shore. It is one of six found periwinkle species covered in this book and present at Ross beach. It comes tagged with a social history, whereby it was once harvested in large quantities by coastal communities, sometimes for domestic use, sometimes for Summer visitors, and as a product it has been harvested and exported to mainland Europe, especially France, Holland and Spain. Wholesale exporters exist around the country and official studies - statistics suggest that annual exports range between 3,000 and 7,000 tonnes per annum. As a 'free for all' harvest-able mollusc, over-fishing has been reported at certain coastal locations.

On Ross beach, the adult periwinkle is distributed throughout the shore and can be found in shallow and deep rock pools at all levels, together with open rock and boulder, in shallow waters, on algae covered lower shore rock, in crevices and under rocks in lower shore areas, as well as under rocks in rock pools. A wide variety of habitats are therefore suitable for this specie and these are all put to use at Ross.

Social (maybe) mating congregation under lower shore rock

Occasionally a striking russet or striped individual may be encountered.

A preference for shingle boulders in shell gravel has been documented

Edible Periwinkle

(Littorina littorea)

While the distribution of **Edible Periwinkle** at Ross is wide and varied across the shore, the density of fully mature individuals is generally not high, and on an average basis, a measurement of 15-20 per square metre of shoreline is probably an accurate estimate. I have not encountered periwinkle pickers on the shore during the times and dates of my research, even though I am aware that periwinkle picking is carried out along the nearby coastline for domestic and commercial purposes.

The Edible Periwinkle has a life span of up to twenty years. There are male and female individuals. The female is fertilized internally before laying capsules of eggs - normally 1-3 - which are released at the time of spring tides. This activity can be ongoing throughout the year and can be influenced by local environmental factors. The periwinkle larvae eventually settle as young periwinkles on the shore, where it takes 12-18 months for them to reach maturity.

The Edible Periwinkle has a relatively cryptic colouration, being dull grey/brown black in colour with a pointed apex. They can look quite similar to the Toothed Topshell on the shore, but the topshell has a much more rounded shell, with a rounded apex and a mottled purplish coloration. They avoid dessication at higher levels of the shore by sealing themselves in by means of an operculum. Predators include crabs, gulls, crows, starfish and humans.

Kilkee

Close by, in the busy tourist resort of Kilkee, Periwinkle and Dillisk traders, provide Limerick and other visitors to Kilkee with a traditional summer experience that stretches back generations and is synonymous with the town. Periwinkles played an important role in the survival of local coastal communities during the Great Irish Famine - 1847 -1852.

Rough Periwinkle & Small Periwinkle

(Littorina saxatilis & Littorina neritoides)

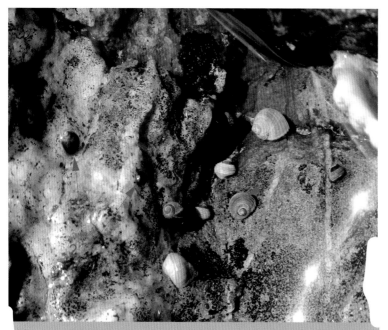

Above - **Rough Periwinkle & Small Periwinkle** in tiny shallow rockpool - uppershore. These juvenile shells measure 5mm or less.

The **Rough Periwinkle** (*Littorina saxatilis*)(1), is much ribbed and rough to the touch. A smaller periwinkle, than the Edible Periwinkle, it is generally colourful, with variations in reds, yellows and greys. Its main location is on the upper shore, often found in crevices or pools with crevices, and is otherwise mostly out of water. It can be found as low as the middle shore. It has developed the ability to breathe out of water. The reproduction process of the Rough Periwinkle differs greatly from *Littorina littorea* (Edible Periwinkle) in that it broods its young in an internal pouch consisting of hundreds of eggs, then releases them as small snails. Another lookalike species often found at this level at Ross is the **Small Periwinkle** *(Littorina neritoides)* (2 & image page 58), which differs from the Rough Periwinkle in that it doesn't have a rough surface but instead a shiny surface and has a longer shelled body, than that of the wider shell of the Rough Periwinkle. These are mostly dull grey in colour, and it takes alot of observation to judge them apart.

Flat Periwinkle
(Littorina obtusata)

Littorina obtusata
Flat periwinkle

1 - This mid - January photo depicts a juvenile Flat Periwinkle - approx size 5mm in a lower shore pool, in the vicinity of many more juveniles. The juveniles tended to be only located at this level on the shore while the adults were more widely distributed throughout all levels. Grazing *Chondrus crispus*.

The Flat Periwinkle *(Littorina obtusata)*is probably the most colourful gastropod on the shore. Empty shells add colour to dead shell assemblages on the shore. It doesn't appear to have a cryptic strategy for survival, however, it has been suggested that because it mainly grazes on the brown wracks *Fucus serratus* and *Fucus vesiculosus* on the lower shore, that when submerged under water and sunlight, these brown wracks actually appear more yellow as the image below of the Serrated Wrack shows. The Flat Periwinkle is found on the Eastern coast of North America and throughout Europe. At Ross it is relatively abundant in its habitat. The female Flat Periwinkle reproduces by laying benthic egg capsules from which young snails hatch. The eggs have been internally fertilized by the male and are laid in gelatinous egg masses on the fronds of the Serrated Wrack. Indeed close examination of this seaweed in March, shows up quite alot of their egg mass. Each egg mass contains approx 100 eggs. The young take 3-4 weeks to pass through this larval stage before biting their way out of the capsule as young snails.

I executed a computer based colour analysis of the Serrated Wrack *(Fucus serratus)*, (left) seen through sunlight, and the Flat Periwinkle *(Littorina obtusata)* (above) which revealed an exact colour match between them close to the apex of the periwinkle. This provides clues as to the reasoning for the bright yellow colouration of this periwinkle, whose favoured diet is the Serrated Wrack.

Flat Periwinkle
(Littorina obtusata)

Egg masses of the Flat Periwinkle laid on *Fucus serratus* (Serrated Wrack) in mid-March. This seems to be a quiet period for the Serrated Wrack, in terms of its usage. I have only observed these egg masses on most of the fronds that I checked. The egg capsules are covered in a jelly like substance and albumen, which feed the larvae and prevent drying out when emersed. Young periwinkles will crawl free in 3-4 weeks.

Below Right: The Serrated Wrack emersed looks much darker, exposing the Flat Periwinkle to its predators when out of water.

There is at least one other member of this Flat Periwinkle group: *Littorina fabalis*, that looks very similar to that of *Littorina obtusata*, so close in fact, that it is very often only possible to identify them by their body organs.

Attractive swirling line formation

Other Periwinkles
(Lacuna spp.)

These little periwinkles may be common at Ross, but I rarely find them. They require very close examination to actually identify them. The Banded Chink Shell has 5 whorls on its shell getting smaller to the apex, while the Tiny Lacuna has three whorls on its shell, which may also be banded, like that of the Banded Chink Shell. These are less well known members of the Periwinkle Family.

Above: The **Banded Chink Shell** (*Lacuna vincta*) on Sugar Kelp .

Above: The **Tiny Lacuna** (*Lacuna parva*) on the lower shore.

Winter Assemblage on lower shore bedrock.

January on the shore

The colourful variation of rock and species in this Winter assemblage, is a depiction of the exquisite detail and beauty that can be experienced at any time on the rocky shore. Above scene depicts a heavily cemented holdfast of the Serrated Wrack (*Fucus serratus*), iron oxidized white rock, ribbed Common Limpets (*Patella vulgata*), green *Ulva(spp)*, Flat Periwinkle (*Littorina obtusata),* broken shell fragments.

Shallow Rockpool Assemblage

Upper Shore Shallow Rockpool

An assemblage of living and dead gastropods, shell gravel and bio-coated sandstones on an upper shore rockpool. Of particular interest is the tiny pink **Auger Shell**, (*possibly Turritella communis*), shown at (1) above. I have not found a live individual on the shore or in the sub-tidal, and this is just an empty shell. (2) A cryptic **Blenny** (*Lipophrys pholis*), stands motionless resting on its pectoral fins. Occasional, perhaps abundant, but hidden in the rockpools here, it feeds mainly on shrimp and worms. The Blenny is equipped with an internal rhythm, that prepares it to forage widely during day time high tides, before retreating to its low tide refuge. (3)An iron oxidized sandstone rock, a common and colourful feature on the upper shore pools. Elsewhere, topshells and periwinkles graze side by side.

Rockpool - Common Keyhole Limpet
(Diodora graeca)

Upper shore rock pool

(1) A **Keyhole Limpet** *(Diodora graeca),* measuring approx 2.5cm. This singular dead shell found on an upper shore rock pool, differs visually from the Common Limpet *(Patella vulgata)* by virtue of the fact that it has a small formed hole, at the apex, which is slightly off centre, together with sculpted radial ribs and with concentric ribbing. The Keyhole limpet eats sponges such as the **Breadcrumb sponge**, which are found from the lower shore down into the deep sub-tidal. The top opening is to allow a through channel for water current. These are primitive molluscs that are not closely related to the *Patella*. I have yet to find one of these tiny animals alive. Their distribution is spread from the Mediterranean to the Atlantic north to Britain and is therefore a Southern species.

Rockpool - Glass Prawn
(Palaemon elegans)

Upper shore rock pool
(Mid - October)

(2) **Glass Prawn** *(Palaemon elegans)* Staying still and looking straight at me, The transparent, striped Glass Prawn has adopted a strategy of hanging still in the water. This may show some awareness by the prawn of its cryptic colouration. This specie can be abundant in upper and middle shore rock pools during the Summer months but it is almost completely absent during the Winter, when it is known to migrate off shore. As with all rocky shore assumptions, it is not possible to state that there is a complete absence in Winter as I have photographed one in an upper shore pool in late January. In this rockpool it is sharing food with high living Beadlet Anemones and Hermit Crabs. It may fall prey to either. Its own diet consists of small crustaceans, worms and fish larve/plankton.

Rockpool - Sea Hare
(Aplysia punctata)

Middle Shore Pool - July

1 - An uncommon encounter with a **Sea Hare**(*Aplysia punctata*), an unlikely looking mollusc gastropod (same category as Limpets). During the hot Summer of 2013, this individual made a one day visit to the middle shore, where it is seen here grazing on the not so common Brown Tuning Fork Weed*(Bifurcaria bifurcata)*. The Sea Hare often grazes on red algaes, and this influences its external colouring. Being soft and fleshy (mollusc is internal) The Sea Hare could easily fall prey to all sorts of shore predators from Anemones to Crabs and Lobsters. When threatened, it emits a purple or red dye. It is not known what the purpose of this dye is. Sea Hares are slow moving and have four tentacles on their head, which look like the ears of a hare. These are hermaphrodite creatures each having both male and female organs, and they come together in Summer time for mating rituals. A typical Sea Hare has just a one year life-cycle.

Nudibranch-Sea Slug

(2)Seeing a tiny orange blob through the new growth of the fronds of Carrígeen, on the lower shore in a sheltered cove at the shore during Mid-March, I reach for the camera. It rarely lets me down!. Sometimes, the organisms are so small, I cannot possibly begin to identify them until I get back to base and download the work. If I had known this was the little **Nudibranch Sea Slug** (*Facelina auriculata*), I would have spent more time observing its colourful patterning and its behaviour. These little swimming creatures feed on various hydroids, on the lower shore and shallow sub-tidal, but also live offshore. On this rock at this time, the blob like tiny formations of the **Elegant Anemone** (*Sagartia elegans*), which may also be the purpose of its trip here. The fully grown size of this species of Nudibranch sea slug is approx 38mm.

Rockpool - Hermit Crabs

(Pagurus bernhardus)

December - 2 Hermit Crabs upper shore rock pool

Speeding around in rock pools partially encased in the shell of a whelk, periwinkle or topshell, the **Hermit Crab** appears playful. It is extremely **sensitive to sound** and will retract rapidly into its shell and drag itself under a rock or crevice at lightening speed. Hermit Crabs are quite common in rock pools from gravelly pools on the upper shore to the seaweed clad lower shore pools. As they grow bigger, they need to change into a bigger shell, so they may fight one another for a shell exchange. There was a skirmish going on between the two in the above photo, whereby one had retracted into its shell in defense, and the Flat Periwinkle shell clad crab, was tossing it about before dragging it into a crevice. The Hermit Crab scavenges on detritus, small fish and algae.   It in turn is preyed on by shore birds, crabs and fish at high tides. Hermit Crabs are known to have a long life cycle, with 50-70 years quoted for aquarium individuals, changing shell many times. They can live on freshwater and saltwater and are often kept as pets. There are up to 20 different species found throughout the British Isles. Found at all levels on the shore throughout the seasons.

Other Crabs

Broad-clawed Porcelain Crab (*Porcellana platycheles*)

Common Shore Crab (*Carcinus maenas*)

Edible Crab (*Cancer pagurus*)

Velvet Swimming Crab (*Necora puber*)

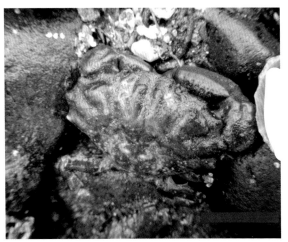

Furrowed Crab (*Xantho incisus*)

Crabs are one of the most distinctive animals found on the shore. They have eight legs two claws, two pairs of antennae and eyes on stalks.

The crab's main defence is a hard shell that covers the whole body. This hard shell is inflexible and so for the crab to grow it has to periodically shed it. This process of moulting is known as ecdysis. This is a time of danger for the crab, as its shell is now soft and requires time to harden. Crabs cases found on shore may be the result of this growing and casting off process.

Crab - strategies - prey and preyed

Crabs - are major predators on the shore, especially from the middle shore down. All species are to be found hiding under boulders, scurrying across rock pools, and are highly sensitive to disturbance. In fact, Crabs themselves, fall prey to a whole host of predators, hence their shore strategy of hiding out. Turning over lower shore boulders to see what may be beneath and underneath, I am often met with various species of crab. Each one has its own strategy. The heavily camouflaged **Velvet Swimming Crab** (*Necora puber*) freezes in situ, perhaps in some way understanding that it can be barely visible against a mottled surrounding of muddied pebble. This particular crab is known to be aggressive, lifting its claws in an aggressive stance, which combined with its red eyes, has earned it the name of 'Red-eyed Devil'. On the lower shore, it is normally juvenile individuals that I encounter, and whilst these juveniles have yet to develop this aggression, their willingness to stay put when disturbed is, perhaps a precursor. The Velvet Swimming Crab can easily be identified on the shore by the 'stripey' lines in its walking legs, combined with its red eyes. It feasts on various molluscs, including mussels, limpets, periwinkles, top shells and dogwhelks. It has thin claws and can extract a periwinkle from its shell without crushing the shell. This it does by catching the leg of the periwinkle with its claws and dragging it out of the shell, thereby leaving an empty shell available for its cousin the Hermit Crab. In this way, the Velvet Swimming Crab and others naturally control populations of *Littorina* on the shore. Velvet Swimming crab is a sought after delicacy in France.

A diverse crab community at Ross Beach.

The **Broad-clawed Porcelain crab**(*Porcellana platycheles*) hides on the lower surface of rock on the lower shore, where there are normally many individuals on the same rock. This is a somewhat different habitat, than being sheltered under a rock. Probably the most cryptic of all crabs, they are not immediately noticeable until they start to crawl quickly to seek refuge from the disturbance of having their rock turned over. For me, it has proved to be a 'task' to get a crisp image of these moving creatures. These crabs are quite tiny, measuring approx 2cm max, and are a dirty muddy colour. It is a scavenger that feeds on detritus and carrion, which it roots out of the gravel and mud around them. This particular crab falls prey to other crabs notably the Edible Crab, the Velvet Swimming Crab and the Furrowed Crab.

When I encounter the much more abundant **Common Shore Crab** (*Carcinus maenas*), underneath a rock, it immediately scurries for cover. This mottled green crab, which can be found on both the North East and North West Atlantic shores, has a serrated edging to its rounded carapace, and can mostly be found from the middle shore to the lower shore during the juvenile stage of their life-cycle. They appear much less common in Wintertime, and it is believed that they move offshore during Winter months. With their strong claws which are thicker than that of the Velvet Swimming Crab, they tend to 'crush' their prey, mostly molluscs, dog whelks, mussels, limpets and periwinkles. Before a shore crab attacks its prey, it decides whether to attack or ignore it. This depends on the size of the prey versus the size of the crab, and smaller crabs will only prey on small mussels and molluscs, as it takes too much energy and less success to crack open those of large fully grown members of its prey.   These crabs are most active during night–time high tides, when they roam throughout the inter-tidal levels.   Research shows that Molluscs such as *Littorina* and *Nucella* have developed narrower openings and thicker shells as a protection mechanism against predation on sheltered shores, where these crabs have greater access to them as prey.

Like the Common shore Crab, the reddish/brown juvenile **Edible Crab** crushes its prey with its claws. It feeds on the same range of prey, and it in turn is equally preyed on by the 'mobile predators' - birds, and fish. It is also a commercial species, widely harvested for human consumption.

Crab predating - Cormorants
(Phalacrocorax carbo)

Mid- Winter

Birds descend on the lower shore at low tide to forage for prey, while fish invade the shore during high tides. Therefore, crabs need to be continuously aware of the threat from predators. The most common bird predators are Oystercatchers, Gulls, Cormorants (outer shore- larger crab prey) and Crows. The **Oystercatchers** descend on the shore, usually in a large group at low tide, where they feast on everything from limpets and crabs to mussels, whelks and periwinkles, They hammer and stab their prey to break the shell and they may eat some species whole. Crows and Gulls are widespread predators, with the ability to control the distribution of up to thirty species of mollusc and crustaceans on the shore. Crabs are often seen with legs missing, this is due to their defence strategy of purposely shedding a leg or claw to a predator. This strategy is known as autotomy. *The above image depicts Cormorants living on the edge of rock on the outer shore at Ross, where they prey on a wide variety of fish and crustaceans heading towards the shore.*

The **Herring Gull** (*Larus argentatus*) together with other members of the Gull and Crow family are major predators on the shore, with the ability to control up to 30 species of shore creatures.

Oystercatchers (*Haematopus ostralegus*) descend on the lower shore at low tide to feast on molluscs, crustaceans and fish. They also occupy nearby fields where they feast on worms and beached ocean kelp laden with tiny creatures and eggs after ocean storms. They tour as a flock. With their long pointed beaks they hammer and stab their prey to break open the shell. Sometimes they eat their prey whole.

Green Starlet
(Asteria phylactia)

Asteria phylactia

The most commonly found starfish at Ross is the **Green Starlet** (*Asteria phylactia*). This spiny coated chubby five armed creature is normally not found in such exposed conditions, foraging amongst Kelps and other seaweeds in the shallow sub-tidal, but instead finding its home beneath rock and boulder anywhere from the upper shore to the shallow waters, being more commonly found at the lower levels. The Cushion Star is a shore predator feasting on small worms, star ascidians and other small encrusting creatues. Its brown cousin the **Cushion Star** (*Asteria gibbosa*) is also found here in smaller numbers. So too is the Common Starfish (*Asterias rubens*).

A selection of 'Worms'

Browsing the shoreline, leaving no stone unturned, one experiences incredible hidden activity. The **Worm Pipefish** (*Nerophis lumbriciformis*) can be found moving about under rock and amongst seaweed on the lower shore. It has a slender eel-like look. It can appear light green to dark brown in colour and is not commonly found at Ross. The species is an Eastern Atlantic species that can be found from Norway to West Africa. The male of the species carries the eggs, for the female who transfers approx one hundred and fifty eggs into a groove in the males body. The eggs are carried between May and August. Another distinctive feature is its long slender snout. This creature is related to the Sea Horses.

(2)This image was taken from the shallow sub-tidal in a sandy gravel section of the shore, the preferred habitat of the **Lugworm** (*Arenicola marina*). The gravel covered cast is indeed just a hint as to the presence of this burrowing worm, which feeds on organic matter ingested with the sediment in which it lives. The Lugworm is itself preyed on by anglers for bait, by wading birds and various fish species.

(3) Although buried in sediment, these slender curled arms are most likely that of the **Slender Brittle-star** (*Amphiura filiformis*), whose arms stretch vertically upwards to filter feed in the water column. This is a long lived species and it is known to have rapid regeneration abilities, being able to regenerate a lost arm within weeks.

(4) Turning over boulders in the sediment rich environment of the shallow sub-tidal at Ross, uncovers a habitat chosen by many organisms ranging from Cushion Stars to the Broad-clawed Porcelain Crab, to a host of worms and organic matter, larvae and eggs. Spoilt for food choice the segmented **Ragworm** (*Hediste diversicolor*), is a burrowing worm, but frequents the underside of boulders when out of its burrow. It is known to be a speedy aggressive hunter and is itself much hunted as bait by anglers. I have not frequently encountered these worms, which may be found in suitable environments throughout North West Europe, but this may be because they are normally in their burrows.

1 - The **Green Leaf Paddleworm** (*Eulalia viridis*) is a very long slender bright green worm which can be found under rocks or on seaweeds in the shallow sub-tidal. Its distinctive green egg nest attaches to the fronds of seaweeds in the Springtime and looks very delicate. See page 94.

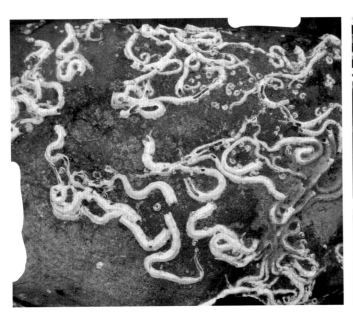

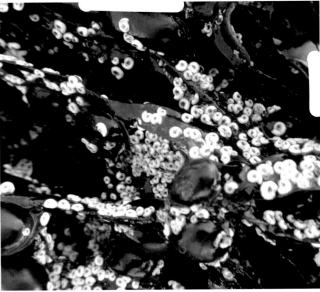

(2) **Keelworm** (*Pomatoceros lamarcki*) lives inside this calcareous triangular tube, which is normally found attached to boulder on the lower shore. This sessile creature is therefore well protected and stretches out its crown of feeding tentacles when submerged in water. These are an abundant species at Ross.

(3) Also abundant and availing of a broader range of habitat is the **Coiled Tube Worm** (*Spirobis spp.*). These are most often found on the fronds of the Serrated Wrack (*F. serratus*)on the lower shore. A smaller variation may also be found in mid Summer, sky-facing, afloat the broad fronded Sugar Kelp (*L.saccharina*). Brooding takes place within the tube.

Simple Creatures - patterned colonial living

(1) **Pattern forming**, colonial living tiny creatures on the rocky shore, add decoration and colour at the tiniest detail level. Like an artist, finishing off a layered work of art, the detail gets smaller and refined with progression. The **Star Ascidians** (*Botryllus schlosseri*) provide this very defined, decorative detail on the rocky shore. To find it, is to train ones eyes to look at the finer detail. These are individually tiny animals known as zooids, but combined may form a star or flower shaped pattern on the back of a frond of Carrigeen, Serrated Wrack, beneath boulders on the lower shore and shallow sub-tidal waters. Within their blob jelly-like sack, the Star Ascidian which is a sessile, filter feeding creature, feeds on plankton and have a shared water circulation and excretory system . These creatures, which are hermaphrodites - each containing male and female reproductive structures - are themselves eaten by Cowries and Star Fish. Star Ascidians may also reproduce asexually by budding and grow their colony quite quickly.

(2) Another pattern forming colonial Ascidian sea squirt probably (*Clavelina lepadiformis*) or **Light bulb Sea Squirt** shares the same seaweed frond. It gets its name from glowing line-drawing like structures that are visible through its transparent body. My experience has been to encounter this species more often in the late Summer/Autumn than at any other time of year.

Simple Creatures - pattern forming colonial living

Exquisite **Star Ascidian** sea squirts *(Botryllus schlosseri) (1)* are tiny colonial creatures that require just a small space like the back or front of a small Carrigeen frond or Serrated wrack frond. One needs to examine these habitats carefully to locate them most likely in the shallow sub-tidal.

Star Ascidian sea squirts *(Botryllus schlosseri)(2)* bring vibrant colour variation as seen in this image combining the red fronds of Carrigeen, Common Green Branched Weed, shelled gravel and filamentous seaweed species, all located in the shallow sub-tidal at Ross.

At the end of Summer, a study of the back of Carrigeen fronds, yields a complete coating in a lace like **Sea Mat** (*Membranipora membranacea*)(3). This normally sub-tidal species, is a complete colony of tiny filter feeding zooids that grow quickly and cast themselves around the stipes of large kelps like Forest Kelp, together with Carrigeen and Serrated Wrack.

Tiny jelly-like beige blobs of developing Sea Squirts *(Aplidium spp.)* (4) may be found throughout the lower shore and shallow sub-tidal on heavily occupied wet surfaces during Spring. Each blob consists of tightly packed zooids. This species is known to have a northern distribution.

Appreciating Autumnal Assemblages

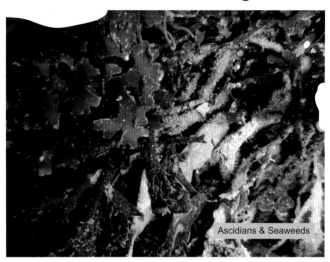

Ascidians & Seaweeds

Anemones, Ascidians & Seaweeds, in their various shapes, forms, colours & textures in mid-Autumn.

Variation of Ascidian & Seaweed life forms - an Autumnal diversity.

Looking into the shallow-sub-tidal in mid Autumn, the density of texture, the variation of colour, the elements of decay and the diversity of sea life all present within the tiny microcosm of the camera lens. Within each tiny segment, one could easily loose a day, maybe more, trying to unravel the mix. Perhaps one should not concentrate on the mix at all, but instead embrace the natural presentations, ascidians, sea anemones, seaweeds, surfaces, for within the next tidal swing, the next light or dark airflow, things will change. It may be predators, turbulence, dullness of light, dispersal or otherwise that will drive the change. If all else remains the same, the brightness and darkness of light generated by the sky will determine ones level of appreciation. Dark skies do not elucidate the sub-tidal well, making it difficult to browse beneath the surface. Light, especially good sunlight, on the other hand shines deep and brings the benthic floor to life.

Just like the trees that surround us show signs of leaf decay, and deciduous properties, all very visible at territorial level, so too, do many of the seaweeds, big and small of the shallow benthic floor, replicate that which happens on land. The difference here, is that few observe such change. Autumn therefore must be seen as more than a terrestrial season, but also a sub-terrestrial season, affecting life-forms on land and sea.

For all the decay aforementioned, there is also semblances of reproduction, with the swollen golden frond tips of the female Carrigeen (*Mastocarpus stellatus*) (1) visible.

Simple Creatures - Sponges & Hydroids

Breadcrumb Sponge

1) The **Breadcrumb Sponge** (*Halichondria panicea),* is a simple animal that lives in sheltered crevices, overhangs and rock pools on the lower shore and shallow sub-tidal. A distinctive, pattern like spotted surface is caused by ex-halent openings which filter out water and waste from the animal. This is a sedentary, encrusting creature, that filters nutrient and oxygen from water currents. It is heterosexual, and therefore has both male and female reproductive mechanisms and its simplicity means that it does not have circulatory, respiratory or digestive systems. Found sporadically throughout the identified habitats, and sometimes it appears as a dull beige colour, especially in Winter. Other times it may present as a rich green colour which is caused by a symbiotic algae living close to its surface.

2) Occupying the same type of habitat as the Breadcrumb Sponge, the Hydroid, **Sea Fir** (*Dynamena pumila*) can be easily overlooked due to its size and dull colouring. This little plant like creature is a stinging predator that also lives a sessile life attached to bedrock or boulder. It is a relation of jellyfish and anemones and is in turn preyed on by sea slugs. The Sea Fir can be seen washed up as high density attachments to the stipes of kelps after ocean storms.

Simple Creatures - Sea Squirts - Ascidians

Shallow sub-tidal

Wading through the shallow sub-tidal, at any time during the year, the abundance of the **White flake Ascidian** *(Aplidium pallidum)* (1) draped over the stipes of **Carrigeen** *(Chondrus crispus)* and **Discoid Fork Weed** *(Polyides rotundus)* ensures that the semi sheltered inner shore at Ross provides a perfect habitat for this simple animal. The **Sea Squirt** *(Didemnid sp)*(2) may easily be confused with the **Purse Sponge** *(Grantia compressa)* whereby each of them have one pronounced exhalent opening, similar colouration and habitat. Seaweeds, such as Carrigeen can be coated with sponges, ascidians, sea mats and encrusting epiphytic seaweeds to an extent that it may be smothering for the host seaweed, and difficult for it to grow and develop as it requires sunlight and direct access to water to make its own food and energy.

Another sessile colony of filter feeding Sea Squirts *(probably Morchellum argus)* (above) living in the sheltered under hang of a large boulder in the shallow sub-tidal. When emersed, the attractive individual zooids are retracted. Sea Squirts living in a colony like this, normally have individual in-halent siphons for taking in water and organic matter and share ex-halent siphons. As a monger for visual detail, I am utterly fascinated by the variety, textures and behaviours of these organisms.

It can be difficult to decipher the many gelatinous or fleshy 'blobs' that appear from time to time on the rocky shore. Always at play and sometimes looking extremely similar are sponges, sea squirts, larvae and egg mass. Telling them apart requires careful examination of both habitat and image, consultation with identity books and online resources, sometimes professional or microscopic assistance.

Competition for space

Lower shore assemblage

The competition for available space greatly increases the further down the shore one travels. In the above late Winter assemblage, a lower shore boulder is completely utilized by a combination of fauna and seaweed. Occupation that stands out, includes that of the **Snakelocks Anemone***(Anemonia viridis),* **Coralline Crusts** (*Lithophyllum & Lithothamniom* spp.*),* the juicy red chained beadlets of the **Bunny-eared Bead Weed** (*Lomentaria articulata),* **Common Green Branched Weed** *(Cladophora rupestris),* tiny hold fasts of **Thong Weed** *(Himanthalia elongata),* **Coiled Tube Worm***(Spirorbis spp),* amongst other inhabitants. This boulder is in its upright position. Generally most seaweeds require light, and therefore they do not inhabit the undersides of boulders - excepting some encrusting species. This scene plays out throughout the Lower shore at low tide.

Competition for space

Beneath boulder - Lower Shore

Competition for space is so intense on this overturned lower shore rock that the shell of **Common Limpe**t (*Patella vulgata*) has been completely covered in a bio mass that includes egg ribbon, worms and Crustose Corraline algae. The **Beadlet Anemone** *(Actinia equina)*, however, remains uncovered, perhaps because of its aggressive predatory strategies or perhaps because of its slippery external mucus coating. Just as the up-facing boulder on the lower shore is a magnet for seaweed species, that require some light for growth, beneath overturned rocks can equally be space competitive for vast quantities of fauna, seeking shelter, refuge and feeding grounds, together with their eggs, and brooding off-spring.

4 REPRODUCTION ON THE SHORE

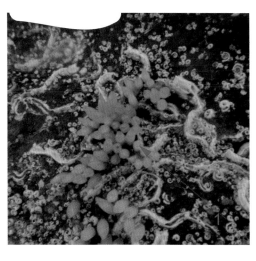
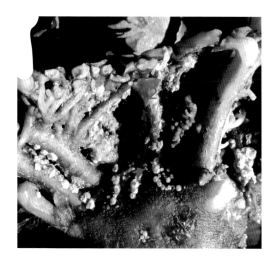
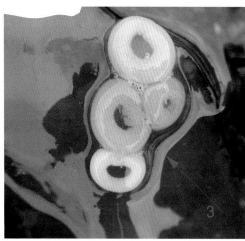
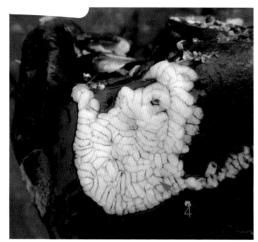

A selection of Egg Capsules

Through my continuous research on the shore, I have been led to a stage of acute awareness as to diversity of habitat. Shore creatures choose habitats as tiny as the frond or stipe of a particular seaweed in which to lay their eggs. The specific habitat could be chosen for a myriad of reasons, including its location on the shore, its chemical cues, mucus coating, its perceived safety from predators, wave action and so forth. The **Common Dog Whelk** (*Nucella lapillus*) lays her eggs (1) beneath rock and boulder on the lower shore. The Egg ribbons of sub-tidal sea slugs on the holdfast of **Forest Kelp** (*Laminaria hyperborea*)(2) The periwinkle gastropod, the **Banded Chink Shell** (*Lacuna vincta*) lay their egg capsules, which swell up over time, very specifically on the fronds of **Sugar Kelp** (*Saccharina latissima*) (3), **Tangle Kelp** (*Laminaria digitata*) and **Serrated Wrack** (*Fucus serratus*), Other sub-tidal living Nudibranch sea slugs, the **Maned Sea Slug** (*Aeolidia papillosa*) choose to deposit their eggs on the underside of lower shore boulders (4). Meanwhile the **Flat Periwinkle** *(Littorina obtusata),* chooses the frond of the **Serrated Wrack** *(Fucus serratus).* Within each attractive circular egg capsule, there may be thousands of tiny eggs, which will eventually release into free swimming larvae or develop directly into juveniles of the species. Larvae will develop further phases before as few as two percent may make it to adult status. The prettiness, formed perfection and variation of these egg capsules on the shore yields a sense of amazement to those who wish to observe such things.

An attractive mint coloured egg sack of the **Green-leaf Paddleworm** (*Eulalia viridis*) attached to the fronds of Carrigeen (*Chondrus crispus*) in the shallow sub-tidal in March. Noting a significant quantity of these egg sacks beautifully woven and hung onto the fronds of Carrigeen and other sub-tidal seaweeds, makes one realize that this is a chosen habitat.

Considering the diversity of flora and fauna living on the shore, it is certain that the reproductive processes undertaken by all these living organisms meet with varying degrees of success. What is hidden here in nature's code, is the sheer ingenuity and breadth of methods, strategic timing, and the stages that occur between fertilization and recruitment into a visible recognisable member of the community. Understanding some of the processes involved brings a whole new meaning and sense of wonderment to the diversity of shore life.

The **Common Limpet** lives throughout the shore with a greater dominance on the middle to lower shore. Here one will normally encounter them in small aggregations, normally numbering eight to twelve. All members of the Common Limpet are born male, and on maturity at approximately nine months, at least one member in a group will change sex to that of female. Triggered by rough Spring tides, between October and February, the female Common Limpet (*Patella vulgata*), releases its unfertilized eggs into high velocity waters. At the same time, possibly triggered by chemical cues, the male releases sperm into the water. The expectation is that the eggs will be externally fertilized in the water column by the male sperm. The fertilized egg transforms into free swimming larvae, morphing into various larval stages while remaining in the water column for some time, possibly several weeks, dispersing and sussing out a suitable

Reproduction on the shore

(1) The frond of the **Serrated Wrack** (*Fucus serratus*) seems to be the favoured choice for the egg laying and egg holding of several species. Indeed the Serrated Wrack is in full use all year around, therefore rendering it a most important habitat for up to one hundred known species. Above are the egg masses of the **Flat Periwinkle** - *Littorina obtusata/fabalis*, found in Mid-March. It takes up to four weeks for crawling young to emerge. They are immediately left to their own devices, with no parental care.

(2) The handsome green doughnut-shaped egg mass of **Banded Chink Shell** - *Lacuna vincta* - a member of the Periwinkle Family - *Littorina*. This little gastropod can be found at low water hiding out on seaweed or low level crevices. While I have found its eggs on the shore in abundance, I have rarely encountered the 'shy' gastropod.

(3) The under boulder eggs of the **Maned Sea Slug** (*Aeolida Papillosa*) are laid in circular movement and can be found on the shore from April-May in pink and white variations.

substrate on which to settle. While this is happening in mid winter, with freezing waters and rough seas, it is actually a timely moment for rock settlement. During the winter, the rocks are at their barest, leaving ample scope for settlement. Walking through the beach during January, seeking out the settlements of baby limpets, I find them mostly settled as singular individuals in tiny crevices, in a group with adult species, and throughout the shore from the middle shore down. At this point, their size measures approx 5mm and their shells are highly ribbed and dark grey. This shell will only begin to grow on settlement of the swimming larvae on rock. The period of time between larval settlement on the rocky substrate, and its metamorphosis into a recognisable juvenile is the period most fraught with danger, as the larvae has lost its swimming ability but has not yet developed a protective mechanism. This metamorphic process happens with great speed, even within a period of a few hours. It is an amazing feat of nature to see these tiny creatures secured and safe against the ravages of vicious ocean storms that occur during this time.

Reproduction on the shore

In the height of Spring, on the edge of the eastern Atlantic and the final fringe of March, bearing great similarity with terrestrial creatures, a bank of new life commences. At anyone time, creatures are in varying stages of the processes necessary to continue the species. In a territory, that is at best difficult, some species have re-acted by adopting more than one method of reproduction. For instance, the **Elegant Anemone** (*Sagartia elegans*), performs a 'budding' reproduction process, together with a secondary process, that generates larvae and independently settling juveniles.

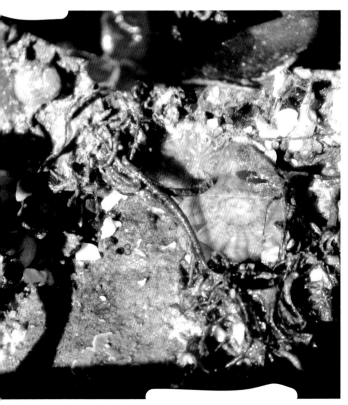

All the time in the world of nature there are predators searching for food. The small egg-shaped gastropod **Cowrie** (*Trivia monacha*), is one such predator (4). Seen here feeding on young developing juveniles of the Elegant Anemone, while the colourful **Nudibranch** slugs also prey on its young. Left to their own devices, these tiny developing sessile creatures use weapons like camouflage, gravel coverage and hiding and must be inherently cued as larvae to protect themselves.

(1) Possibly **White-striped Anemone** - (*Actinothoe sphyrodeta*), *(2)* **Elegant Anemone** *(Sargartia elegans) (3)* **Gem Anemone** *(Aulactinia verrucosa)*, (4)**European Cowrie** *(Trivia monacha)*

Later in spring, the heterosexual **Barnacle** (*Chthamalus sp.*), which lives inside its six plated exo-skeletal crust and is one of the most common animals on the shore, internally fertilizes those other members within its range and may itself be internally fertilized by means of an extensible penis by another. It is therefore important that the Barnacles are closely settled together, as singular Barnacles will not have the opportunity to reproduce. The fertilized eggs are then released as free swimming larvae into the water column, where they will spend some weeks morphing through various stages of development. It is believed that the Barnacles contain sensory abilities that help them to choose exactly the substrate most suitable for settlement. This allows them to choose textured rocks and crevices, which are particularly suitable for holding power, or settlement near adult congregations. Once the larvae settles, it quickly develops an exo-skeleton to protect it from predators and the elements. In early June approx three months later, these baby Barnacles are measuring approx 5mm.

The **Dahlia Anemone** (*Urticina felina*) lives in lower shore rock pools and sub-tidally to 100m deep. It can be a highly variable species with different colour combinations. This anemone, is known to have two methods of reproduction, sexual and asexual. Asexual reproduction occurs where no recombination of genetic material takes place, and the end result is a 'clone' two creatures with the exact same genetic make up. The Dahlia will hence pull itself apart, by a process called '**longitudinal fission**', making two mature individuals from one larger individual. This process takes a couple of days. Hence on locating a grouping of Dahlia or indeed other species of this family that are tightly packed with no colour variation, it is most likely that asexual reproduction has taken place. Biologists have considered the fact that this type of reproduction may occur to enhance feeding opportunities, (two mouths are better than one), when it comes to sourcing prey, and can be a direct response to under nourishment.

The male **Edible Periwinkle** (*Littorina littorea*), may have difficulty recognising the female of the species. This is because there are four closely related members of the *Littorina* species. Males of the *Littorina littorea*, will follow the mucus trail of the female during the mating season. After internal fertilization occurs, the female will then broadcast spawn egg capsules, that release free swimming larvae. On the other hand the golden coloured **Flat Periwinkle** (*Littorina obtusata*) lays benthic egg capsules during the Spring on the leaves of the **Serrated Wrack** *(Fucus serratus)*from which juveniles hatch. Another incredible feature of the shore in deepest winter is to see these tiny 5mm shells surviving the rigours of the ocean, clasping onto fronds of Carrigeen and Wracks. These tiny creatures receive no parenting, and have to learn survival tactics quickly. Displaying an even greater range of reproduction method within this group, the **Rough Periwinkle** (*Littorina saxatilis*) broods its young internally, releasing them as small snails.

In another fascinating reproductive strategy among shore creatures, the male crustacean, the **Edible Crab**, (*Carcinus maenas*), carries a female around on its back until she moults (sheds her hard carapace). At this point copulation takes place and the female carries her eggs beneath her body for several months before being released as larvae into the ocean. She is protected by the male until her soft body hardens with a new carapace.

Seaweed reproduction provides its own fascinating and individualized stories and I have chosen to provide the visual semblances and detail with each species covered in this book, where possible.

5 SEAWEEDS & SEASONS

A global view

The world's oceans are awash with in excess of 10,000 species of Seaweeds. These seaweeds thrive in different types of habitat, in different climates, and in different ocean and seas. Factors, such as access to light, heat, substrate and wave action influence which seaweeds grow in a particular coastline or ocean. Seaweeds are both ecologically and commercially important sea plants, that make food and grow through photosynthesis, similar to land plants. In turn they provide fodder for grazing shore and offshore animals like Limpets (*Patella sp.*) and Periwinkles (*Littorina sp.*). They provide refuge for a host of tiny sea animals and the eggs of many sea slugs are safely deposited in the holdfasts of larger species. Commercially, seaweed such as **Carrígeen** (*Chondrus crispus*) and **Nori (Sliocháin)(Laver)**(*Porphyra*) are cultivated in off shore aqua-culture farms in south east Asia and off the east coast of Canada. Both of these seaweeds and many others are extremely important foods in the human food chain. Aqua-culture is still in its infancy in Europe, however the Irish Government and others are looking at ways at promoting seaweed cultivation for use across several industries.

As with all plants, seaweeds are classified into family groupings. The largest group contains the Red Seaweeds, which includes popular species such as **Dillis**k and **Carrígeen**. The Red Seaweeds are the oldest seaweeds on earth, which according to fossil records, stretch back over a billion years. The Brown Seaweed group contain the largest seaweeds on the planet. These are known as the Kelps, and live in the sub-tidal in habitats known as Kelp Forests.

Late January Assemblage - lower shore

Late January and early signs of Spring emerge on the lower shore boulders with the return of new growth of the green **Sea lettuce** (*Ulva lactuca*), which has been noticeably absent during the Winter months. The circular disks of the biennial species **Thong Weed** (*Himanthalia elongata*), have already made progress from their tiny vegetative buttons that can be seen lingering most of the year. There is also fresh young growth of the red seaweed **Dillisk**(*Palmaria palmata*), which will form part of its abundant offering at Ross.

Kelp forests have the ability to slow down speed of water flow nearing the shore, however they are also liable to be uprooted by rough tides and landed on the shore, often with holdfast still attached to rock.The Green seaweeds, number the smallest group of species, and they can often be found in fresh water, brackish water, and their growth pattern often resembles that of land plants.

Seaweeds at Ross Beach

Over the past number of years, much of my research focus has been on the seaweeds at Ross Beach. Honestly, I became mesmerized with the sheer variety of species, the uniqueness of each species and their growth patterns throughout the year. It was a slow process of elucidation, but every new fragment of knowledge garnered was completely cherished. Researching seaweeds on the beach necessitated my presence there right throughout the year, more so than the creatures. My

January Rockpool, middle shore, the Carrígeen (*Chondrus Crispus*) has taken on a deeper red hue, from the lack of sunshine over the past months. However, new signs of growth are emerging which can be seen on the blue iridescent tip, its energy making process. The evergreen and ever available Green Branched Weed (*Cladophora spp.*) is delicate and attractive, whilst the orange blob in the background is that of the ElegantAnemone (*Sagartia elegans*), who migrates/is transported upshore from the sub-tidal during the months of December to March.

photographic records continually improved with time, as seaweeds can be difficult to capture digitally because of their lingering half in and half out of water, being flopped when out of water and buoyed by air bladders in some cases. Observation skills had to be honed into exact positioning, type of preferred substrata, colour changes, characteristics of reproduction, reaction to exceptional weather conditions such as ice and frost, variation and spread of habitat for a particular species and commencement of growth season. The growth season amongst species probably varied the greatest.

Defining Seaweeds

Generally speaking, the diversity of seaweeds, is accompanied by a diversity of form. It may be surprising to many, that some 'flat coloured surfaces' encountered on the rocky shore are actually seaweeds. These are called encrusting seaweeds, or paint seaweeds. Knobbly surfaces are called crustose encrusting seaweeds.

Late February Scene

Despite the early nudging of growth shown earlier, this overall February scene is one of scarcity over abundance, with the absence in particular of the summertime abundanance of the long strappy seaweed **Thong Weed** (*Himanthalia elongata*), the absence of **Sea Grass** (*Ulva compressa*), and many other species that will rapidly and vigorously inhabit this sub-tidal zone over the coming months. The gravelly sea floor is clearly visible.

At the other end of the spectrum, the large rod-like landings on the shore after rough tides are the Kelp seaweeds. The high density canopy forming Kelp Forest can become like a deciduous forest over the winter months, because of ocean turbulence. Most seaweeds fall into the foliose category, seaweeds that have leaf-like structures called **fronds**. Within this foliose group, fronds are classified by their formation of branching fronds similar to that of the leaves of land plants (opposite, paired, whorled irregular etc). Many but not all seaweeds are attached to substrata, via a structure called a **holdfast** which can be disk-like or claw-like or button-like. It can be fascinating how tightly fastened these holdfasts are, and are typically cemented by calcification onto the rock/boulder surface, particularly the older perennial species. On occasion, I have lifted large rocks by the seaweed on top - especially the Serrated Wrack, without any damage to the seaweed. Unlike land plants, the holdfast (root) of the seaweed does not draw in nutrients and is merely an anchoring system. Many seaweeds, especially Summer species can be encountered free floating, but those attached by a holdfast require to be lifted off the rock when in the water, and so just above the holdfast is a stem-like structure called a **stipe**. Its purpose is to help stand up the seaweed when in water, help it to sway in the water column, without being bashed against the substratum. Seaweed habitat varies widely. On the one hand, there are species, that occupy rock pools on the upper shore, while others prefer out of water living, on the rock formations, only encountering sea water at high tide levels.

Early April Shingle Scene - looking downshore

By early April, an immediate spectacular change is visible on the shore with the greening of the lower shore shingle in a smooth **Sea Grass** (*Ulva spp.*), which will gradually grow over the forth coming months into long flattened tubular fronds. This seaweed is absent from the shore from November to March.

Late September - Looking Upshore

A spectacular feast of colour, form and texture, pervades this late September image taken looking upshore. The green *Ulva spp.* has not only grown into long stringy fronds, but deepened its colour and is now beginning to detach leaving behind it brown patches on the shingle surface which will emerge again next season.

SEAWEED STRUCTURES

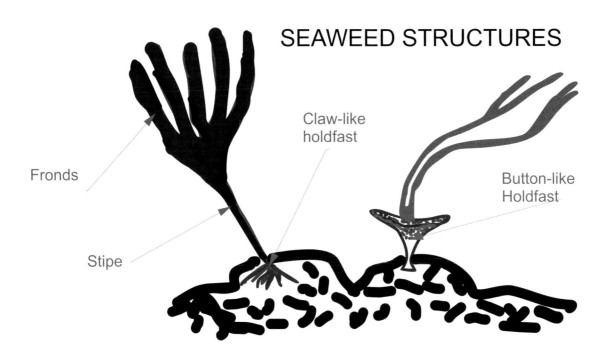

Fronds

Stipe

Claw-like holdfast

Button-like Holdfast

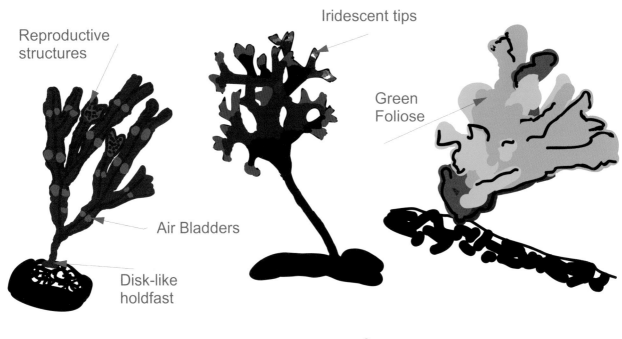

Reproductive structures

Air Bladders

Disk-like holdfast

Iridescent tips

Green Foliose

Plate-like seaweed

Stalked Airbladders

Comparative Assemblage

The images on the opposite page are of the same rock from the lower shore/shallow sub-tidal taken three months apart. A comparative analysis of these images reveals significant evidence of seasonal variation. The image taken on March 1, reveals a complete absence of the green seaweed, **Sea Lettuce** (*Ulva lactuca*), **Punctured Ball Weed** (*Leathesia difformis*) and only young growth of **Bunny-eared Bead Weed** (*Lomentaria articulata*). In addition, **Thong Weed** (*Himanthalia elongata), has* just commenced its seasonal growth. Three months later and the same shore boulder depicts an entire skirting with the now long strappy **Thong Weed** (*Himanthalia elongata*), together with a diverse combination of lower shore/sub-tidal species including **Sea Lettuce** (*Ulva lactuca*), **Bunny-eared bead Weed** (*Lomentaria articulata*), **Pepper Dulse** (*Osmundea pinnatifida)*, among others. This image depicts a Spring into Summer growth season, that at least matches that of land plants.

Early Summer - Splash Zone

Form, Texture, Colour

Meanwhile, late May on the upper shore/splash zone, and indeed one of the prettiest times to visit, and the spring green colour of the **Gutweed** (*Ulva intestinalis*), fills a natural rock channel pool. This orderly containment contradicts the normal 'free for all' living behaviour of shore species. The Gutweed is a year round seaweed, that thrives on the upper shore, where it can sustain low salinity levels. However, in Spring, with the assistance of the sun, it regenerates into a bright green colouring, from its dull dark green Winter colouring, thereby providing an attractive backdrop for the **Sea Pinks** that flower at this time.

Mid-July - shallow sub-tidal

Mid July and the shallow sub-tidal that lay vacant at the end of February, is now brimming with Summer species, including the fully stretched, edible and attractive **Thongweed** (*Himanthalia elongata*), together with an epiphytic specie (*Ceranium pedicellatum*), forming pom poms on top of the Thongweed fronds, **Sea Grass** (*Ulva compressa*), now fully grown, lighter coloured **Carrigeen** (*Chondrus crispus*). Beyond the Thongweed, **Japanese Wireweed** (*Sargassum*), floats to the surface. The warm summer conditions provide a perfect environment for its rapid invasion. Nestled amongst the Seaweeds, the **Black Sea Cucumber** (*Holothuria forskali*) and grazing winkles.

September - landed species

Texture & Formation

September/October, masses of Summer/annual species begin to detach and dessicate, as their natural cycle nears an end. Coupled with uprooted species from the Kelp forest just beyond the shallow-sub-tidal, they float inward with the tide, remain on the shore until the next tide, where they may be collected again and taken back out. This process repeats itself day after day, week after week, as the cache of seaweed desiccates into organic dietrus, making the sub-tidal zone, untidy and debris ridden. Eventually they will get lashed high up on the shore during a rough spring tide, beyond the high tides regular limits, where they will further decay into dried pulp, be fed on by **Kelp Flies**, maybe collected for fertilizer and so forth. If the rough tide does not come, they will eventually decompose from this inward-outward cycle, aided by various creatures who eat decaying matter. This decayed matter provides nutrient enrichment to the ocean waters, which will benefit next years growth of flora and fauna.

Autumn is a great time, to wander through the landed seaweeds, which provide such variety, textures, colours and an opportunity to locate a new species. Amongst the seaweed debris, little creatures, like **Star Ascidians** (*Botryllus schlosseri*) and **Sea Mats** (*Membranipora membranacea*) remain attached to fronds, whilst the **Blue-rayed Limpet** (*Helcion pellucidum)* moves off its kelp home in advance of the shore landing. This cycle plays out year after year, sometimes initiated by rough seas.

Late September - landed species

Biomass & Diversity

The bulkiness of the landings is caused by the large kelps, especially **Sugar Kelp**(*Saccharina latissima*), an annual species which is very abundant here, **Tangle Kelp** (*Laminaria digitata*), normally found in the extreme lower shore/shallow sub-tidal, **Furbellows Kelp** (*Saccorhiza polyschides)*, a large distinctive Kelp that can grow up to 2 metres, and has a distinctive warty holdfast and a strap-like stipe. Also found in this cache an abundance of the red **Dillisk** (*Palmaria palmata*) often attached to the stipe of the **Forest Kelp**(*Laminaria hyperborea*), **Sea Beech** (*Delesseria sanguinea*) and a huge variety of small free floating Summer species. The overall scene is, textured, muted and brings home the incredible beauty and diversity of shore and near shore seaweeds. This bounty should be seen as natures free gift to the land, yet it is a gift that remains ignored, rejected, left on the shore to decay.

Late October - Decay - Shallow Sub-tidal

Above: This late October image taken from the shallow sub-tidal, from an assemblage of flora and fauna that are attached to bedrock or seaweed, depicts an untidy level of decay amongst the seaweed species, while the filter feeding **Star Ascidians**(*Botryllus schlosseri*) look very healthy. Their future may be somewhat unsure, if their host seaweed decays fully. Full year seaweeds may be smothered and compromised by such a heavy coating of living organisms on their fronds and stipes. The whole scale decay of annual seaweeds at this time filters decaying particles into the water column, making visibility generally poor.

For all the decay going on, there are also semblances of reproduction. The swollen tips of the Carrigeen, *(Mastocarpus stellatus)* (1) are entirely visible as sea life on the rocky shore provides a continuous cycle of succession, regeneration and expansion of species.

All year around - Serrated Wrack
(*Fucus serratus*)

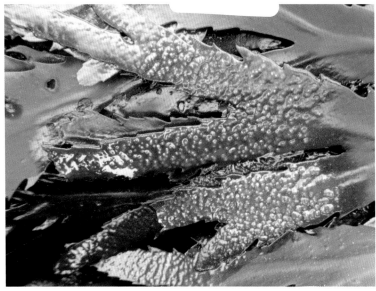

(1) Very distinctive serrated edges are always evident.
(2) Reproductive structures give a bumpy golden appearance.

The **Serrated Wrack** (*Fucus serratus*), is one of the most commonly found, resourceful, brown wracks on the lower shore and shallow-subtidal. It may also be found on lower shore rock pools. You may find it growing on rock formations, or boulder, attached firmly by a discoid holdfast. This ever present seaweed is also one of the toughest. The holdfast is heavily calcified onto its base, and lifting the wrack by its fronds with a heavy rock attached makes no impact on the seaweed. It can withstand severe storm and this has been proved during recent storms,(2014), as despite its precarious positioning in the direct line of the ocean, there was little of the seaweed uprooted from its rock. The Serrated Wrack is an extremely important habitat and host. Depending on the time of year one finds it, it will be playing 'safe haven' and /or 'food supplier', all the time allowing itself to

All year around - Serrated Wrack (*Fucus serratus*)

(1) Growing in the shallow sub-tidal in summertime, an epiphytic seaweed - Tiny Wrack Bush (*Elachista fucicola*) thrives on its flat surface.

(2) The discoid holdfast of the Serrated Wrack is extremely well fastened and can withstand extensive ocean trauma.

(3) In the Autumn - a festooning of simple animals occupy the fronds, causing stress, as the seaweed cannot perform its photosynthesis and may be smothered.

be decorated and coated with other living organisms. For much of the year the white coloured calcareous **Coiled Tube Worm** (*Spirobis* spp*),* coats much of the distinctive serrated fronds and stipe, while in Summer a tiny epiphytic seaweed - **Tiny Wrack Bush** (*Elachista fucicola*) grows atop its fronds in the shallow sub-tidal. In the Autumn and Winter, both sides of its fronds may be festooned with simple animals like **Star Ascidians**(*Botryllus schlosseri*), **Sea Squirts** (*Ascidiella aspera*) and **Sea Mats**(*Membranipora membranacea*). All this coverage puts pressure on the plant, disallowing photosynthesis to take place if the plant is completely coated. The grazers, like the **Flat Periwinkle** that frequently graze its surface therefore provide an important service, that of keeping its surface clear from certain smothering infestations. In the Spring, the Flat Periwinkle (*Littorina obtusata*) lays its eggs atop its fronds. From a human perspective, Serrated Wrack is harvested for various uses in the cosmetic industry, ranging from seaweed baths to seaweed based cosmetics. The Serrated Wrack, like many other seaweeds, has a deep brown/black hue during winter, and an olive hue during Summer. When the sun shines through its fronds it changes colour to a golden yellow therefore providing perfect camouflage for the Flat Periwinkle.

The Serrated Wrack has both male and female individuals, and when in reproductive mode during late Winter into Spring, the frond surface - towards the tips become golden and swollen giving a bumpy texture to the seaweed. Eggs and sperm are released into the water column where fertilization and widespread distribution takes place. Typical life span 3-4 years and this wrack prefers a sheltered to semi-exposed shore and is therefore abundant at Ross.

All year around - Dillisk
(*Palmaria palmata*)

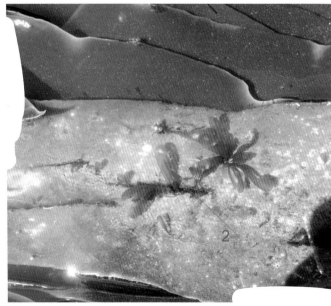

1. Dillisk attached to Bedrock on the lower shore, broad-fronded, and abundant.
2. Young growth on decaying kelp frond - mid Spring.
3. Cloud-like reproductive spores on the frond - August

Also known as **Dulse - Dillisk** a broad and flat fronded, robust purplish /maroon coloured seaweed which is found free-floating, attached to bedrock or to the stipes of kelps. It is abundant at Ross and is a useful and a valuable commercial seaweed. Dillisk is much favoured by the local community, with a long history of usage associated with it. My mother Mrs. Mai Magner, passing Ross beach on her way to primary school in the 1920s/30s stopped by the beach, if the tide was out to collect some for lunch at the school. She still favours its salty taste now in her mid 90s, so I am obliged to collect a little 'treat' for her on many of my shore trips. Although, Dillisk is available on the shore right throughout the year, the young new Spring growth, is deemed to have a more delicate texture and salty flavour. In the height of Summer, larger

All year around - Dillisk (*Palmaria palmata*)

A favourite habitat - young Dillisk can be found amongst the stipes and holdfast of the **Forest Kelp** (*Laminaria hyperborea*). During severe ocean storms an inordinate amount of the seaweed may be lost due to the uprooting of this kelp by the ocean.

batches of Dillisk are collected and spread out under the sun, to bleach and dry. This dried Dillisk is then stored for Winter consumption for the household.

During the Famine era, coastal people who had access rights to Ross beach, collected and ate Dillisk, which according to *Dr. Prannie Rhatigan's* book '**Irish Seaweed Kitchen**' provides a good source of protein, minerals and vitamins, low in sodium and high in potassium. This seaweed also contains **Kainic Acid**, which is known to kill worms. It has been used in this way by humans and administered to animals over the centuries and long before scientists discovered this valuable property. However, this usage was sporadic and limited to communities, where such a belief existed. A wide spread knowledge of this particular fact could have greatly assisted the many coastal farmers who suffered widespread loss of farm animals due to liver-fluke and other worm infestations.

Dillisk is now a commercially licenced harvested seaweed, with the Wild Irish Sea Vegetable Company among others, hand collecting, drying and packaging it directly from the shore for both home and export markets. It is also available in a condiment form, for flaking over soups, salads or as an ingredient in scones and even ice-cream.

Dillisk has played an important role in our history and our diet, is rich in valuable properties and given that it lends itself well to commercial aqua-culture, provides an opportunity for coastal communities to significantly increase commercial value added opportunities by tank based and out at sea cultivation of the species. Currently less than 100 tonnes of wild Dillisk are harvested. European demand for seaweed is miniscule compared with that of South East Asia.

Each Dillisk plant, which is a perennial, generating new frond growth each year, is either male or female, with the male individuals being the ones normally encountered on the shore, while the female is a small crust-like plant. The complicated reproductive cycle takes place between November and April. Major interesting studies, which are accessible online, have been conducted by BIM and others as to its feasibility as a commercial aqua-culture crop with value added processing.

All year around - Egg Wrack
(*Ascophyllum nodosum*)

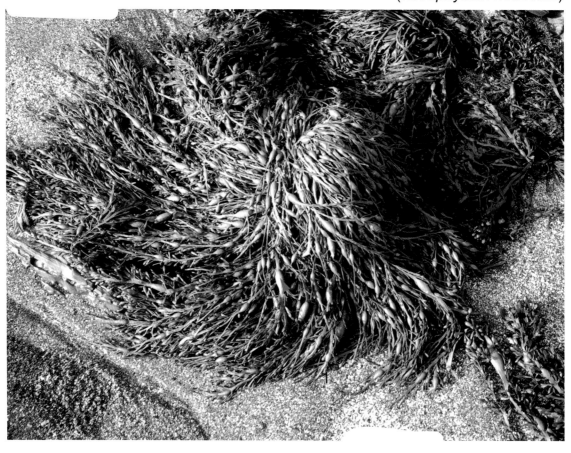

This middle to lower shore brown wrack inhabitant at Ross beach, generally prefers very sheltered sites, and is not particularly abundant here. This seaweed, which is the most actively hand harvested commercial seaweed in Ireland (25,000+ tonnes p.a), is distinctive with its egg shaped air bladders which allow it to float upright when submerged. It grows one air bladder per year, and therefore it is possible to tell its age on the shore. There are male and female individuals and golden yellow swollen oval reproductive structures appear on the male, looking most swollen during the spring when reproduction takes place by release of egg and sperm into the water column.

Traditionally, this has been the best seaweed to harvest for fertilizer and when combined with nettles in a dark storage tank for a number of weeks yielded a high quality, field ready fertilizer. It is now mostly harvested sustainably on sheltered shores in **Connemara**, for use as a meal for cattle and for fertilizer products and export.

1 - A mature Egg Wrack plant, lays flopped down when emersed and floats upright when submerged aided by its air bladders.

2 - The Egg Wrack is normally inhabited by a red seaweed epiphyte, **Wrack Siphon Weed** (*Polysiphonia lanosa*), which burrows into the wrack.

3 Male reproductive structures - mid-April

All year around at the top of the shore

A trio of seaweeds from the top of the shore that are always present:

1 The distinctive mid-ribbed **Spiraled Wrack** (*Fucus spiralis*) lives attached to bedrock on the upper shore just below the splash zone. It prefers a sheltered habitat. It does not have air bladders but it does have the most attractive swollen reproductive structures, which are mostly evident during the Autumn. Its fronds twist and spiral and hence its name.

2 The only splash of Winter green on the shore is most often provided by the tubular **Gutweed** (*Ulva intestinalis).* This can be found fringing upper shore pools, or attached to bedrock. It can tolerate low salinity levels, and its green shading is much darker in the Winter than in Summer and it is often bleached white by extremely hot sunny conditions.

3 **Chanel Wrack** (*Pelvetic canaliculata)*, a small brown tufted wrack will only be found on upper shore bedrock, right throughout the year. It is tolerant therefore of all sorts of weather conditions, and can be blackened by icy conditions, however this is on the outer side only.

4) The reproductive structures of the Spiraled Wrack are distinctive, attractive and mostly found during the Autumn from late July. Each individual is both male and female.

5) The swollen reproductive frond tips of Chanel Wrack normally appear later in the Autumn - October onwards. Each individual is both male and female.

All year around at the top of the shore

The swollen reproductive structures of the **Spiraled Wrack** are most attractive during the months of July to September. They commence growth in January and the structures are shed by November leaving just a flat mid-ribbed spiral forming frond. There are no known uses for Spiraled Wrack at this time. Its favoured location is that of a sheltered shore attached to bedrock just below the Lichen zone, away from most of the grazing community.

1 - Reproductive Structures of Spiraled Wrack (*Fucus spiralis*)(August)

2 - Channel Wrack & its swollen reproductive tips (September)

3 - Prolonged - freezing during Winter blackens the Channel Wrack, but it regenerates.

It is known that **Channel Wrack** can survive for up to eight days when out of water. This is aided by a grooved longitudinal channel curved inwards that helps the plant to retain moisture. The distribution of Channel wrack is confined to the north East Atlantic from the Faroes to Portugal. It is known that this seaweed, which is edible, has been grazed further up the coast by sheep wandering onto the coastline.

All year around at the top of the shore - Gutweed

Gutweed (*Ulva intestinalis*), which is related to other green seaweeds including **Sea Lettuce**, can be found on location at the top of the shore right throughout the year, and survives well in brackish and low salinity waters. During the Winter months it takes on a dull dark green hue, but this livens up in Spring time, there at (1) above its late May bright colouring provides a beautiful backdrop for the odd bunch of **Sea Pinks** that live in its midst. With prolonged periods of sunshine however, the seaweed can be bleached to white, and evidence of bleaching is beginning to show at (2) above, an image taken during early August. The fronds of Gutweed are long tube like fronds and the only time I have seen it being used was in **Masterchef Ireland**, where it was quickly deep fried to provide an 'artistic' garnish for a fish dish!

Gutweed is a short lived specie, normally less than one year, but frequent reproduction, peaking during the Summer months ensures rapid replacement of the species stock.

All year around throughout the shore - Carrigeen
(Chondrus crispus, Mastocarpus stellatus)

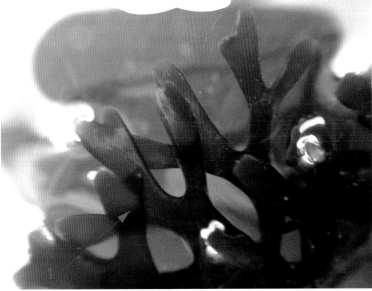

(1) - Carrigeen - *Chondrus crispus - Mastocarpus stellatus* - an important ecological host and commercial seaweed.

Carrigeen - Irish Moss - (*Chondrus crispus*), (*Mastocarpus stellatus*), is one of those seaweeds that conjure up a sense of tradition and social history in our area. Known, used and understood to some degree by the local community, it was in fact locally harvested for commercial purpose. This was part of the entrepreneurial repertoire of Mary Carmody (nee Bermingham), who hand picked, dried, bleached and bagged the seaweed from Fodera and Ross beaches for the local market in Kilrush, where she laid it on a linen clad table and sold it very rapidly. My mother Mai Magner (nee Fennell) and her neighbours Maggie Fennell (nee Lillis) and Mai Blake (nee Fennell) also collected Carrigeen for domestic use.

(2) - Carrigeen - fully grown and appearing bountiful throughout the shore from late April. Each year it regenerates from old stipes and fronds which have remained dormant over Winter months. New growth commences as early as January and upper shore pool living specimens may be the first to 'sprout' during temperate winters.

All year around throughout the shore - Carrígeen

(*Chondrus crispus, Mastocarpus stellatus*)

(1) A young Carrigeen plant, commences growth at the bottom of a rock pool. Carrigeen has distinctive and exquisite tips which have iridescent colouring when viewed at certain angles in good light under water.

During the month of May, they collected the now flourishing Carrigeen from Ross beach, took it to the open moors at Ross, where it was spread out and left to bleach over short grass. It was then collected and bagged. It was boiled with water for cattle feed during the lean times of World War ii, when meal was difficult to come by and it was boiled with milk and egg, strained and flavoured with sugar for home consumption. It appears that their approach to picking the seaweed was non-sustainable however, as they had to 'pluck off' the roots (holdfast) on taking it home. Plucking Carrigeen in this way, is actually removing the plant for good. Carrigeen was seen as an important seaweed for treating chesty colds and flu. Currently the Wild Irish Sea Vegetable Company commercially harvests Carrigeen among other seaweeds for the domestic Irish and Export markets.

(2) Meeting Carrigeen on the shore at various times of year or at varying vertical locations, one is presented with a different array of colours. In the Winter, it is always dark red, no matter where one locates it. In early Summer, on the lower shore, when it looks at its best, it has distinctive golden colouring on the outer parts of the fronds, meanwhile, during sunny Summer months, it appears almost bright green in colour in shallow rock pools at the top of the shore. Carrigeen is the common name used to combine two species *Chondrus crispus* and *Mastocarpus stellatus,* similar but different species. It is for instance known that *Mastocarpus stellatus* is prone to frost, whereas *Chondrus crispus* is much hardier. One is deemed 'coarser' than the other.

All year around throughout the shore - Carrigeen

(Chondrus crispus, Mastocarpus stellatus)

Reproductive structures of female Carrigeen in Spring

The importance of Carrigeen

For Centuries, in many countries throughout the world, **Carrígeen, Irish Moss** (*Chondrus crispus, Mastocarpus stellatus*) was used in jellies and milk puddings. An old receipe for Blanc Mange (Smith 1905):

"Soak half a cup of dry moss in cold water for five minutes, tie in a cheesecloth bag, place in a double boiler with a quart of milk and cook for half an hour; add half a teaspoonful of salt or less, according to taste, strain, flavor with a teaspoonful of lemon or vanilla extract as desired, and pour into a mold or small cups, which have been wet with cold water; after hardening, eat with sugar and cream."

Various modern day possibilities arise for its domestic usage with fruit variations, and exotic flavourings. Carrigeen lends itself to experimentation in this regard. Personally, I enjoy it in a blackberry mouse, served with ice-cream. However, beyond its general low usage level by coastal communities throughout Ireland, it is rarely a sought after product by inland communities. Sadly, its availability is generally limited to some health food stores.

Carrageenan is a polysaccharide substance that is extracted from a variety of red seaweeds, especially Carrigeen (*Chondrus crispus, Mastocarpus stellatus*). These have gelling, thickening and binding, properties, and can be found in many products including ice-cream, toothpaste, chocolate products, meats, desserts and so forth. A very wide and ever increasing application. Carrageenan is a safe food additive according to the Joint Expert Committee on Food Additives assigning it to a group 'acceptable daily intake - not specified', a coding assigned to products that do not represent a health hazard.

Carrigeen lends itself to commercial growing and harvesting, with Canada and the Philippines leading the way. In the warm waters surrounding the Philippines, a variety of Carrageenan seaweeds have portions of their plant laid out on nylon ropes and held in position in their normal habitat in the sub-tidal. Some months later, the crop is hand harvested. Larger aqua-culture developments, lead to harvesting by dredges attached to boats and I have encountered it harvested by dredges attached to horses on youtube. Carrigeen needs to be bleached and dried before packaging for the marketplace. In Ireland, harvesting of Carrigeen is on a very small scale with less than 10 tonnes per annum hand collected from natural stocks. China, Korea and Japan are the main seaweed consuming countries in the world, this represents a high percentage of the total world population. The demand is generally for dried seaweed product. It would be wonderful to see a Carrageenan demand, producing and export industry expand in Ireland.

In its habitat, Carrigeen hosts many sub-tidal creatures, many of the images featured in this book, show the Carrigeen fronds and stipes hosting encrusting seaweeds, ascidians, sea mats and others. Its continuous presence, its sturdy disk-like holdfast, its general distribution throughout the shore and its tolerance of low salinity ensures its diversity as a host plant.

As aforementioned Carrigeen is a term that has been used interchangeably between two species *Chondrus crispus* and *Mastocarpus stellatus*. However closely they may appear in their foliose phase, they each have distinctive reproductive processes. In the case of *Mastocarpus stellatus*, a primary phase in the plants life is that of a dark encrusting algae that can live up to ninety years in this phase before developing a fronded foliose phase. In addition the frond tips of the female *Mastocarpus stellatus* develop swollen pips at the end of their fronds. In the case of *Chondrus crispus*, the female plant forms slight oval shaped swellings approx 2mm in diameter on the fronds.

All year around - Common Green Branched Weed
Cladophora rupestris

(1) **Common Green Branched Weed** (*Cladophora rupestris*) - a pretty, much branched deep green coloured seaweed that can be found in lower shore rockpools and in the shallow sub-tidal, offering an interesting form and colour distraction from the mainly brown and red species found at this level. This late Summer image of this densely populated rock pool also boasts species like the **Serrated Wrack** (*F. serratus*), **Dumont Tubular Weed** (*Dumontia cortorta*), **Coral Weed** (*Corralina officinalis*), *Ulva spp.*, **Edible Periwinkle** (*Littorina littorea*), among others.

During winter months, the Common Green Branched weed, loses some of its vitality and can look a dirty green/olive colour. This can be due to a coating of diatoms (single celled organisms related to the brown seaweeds). The seaweed is wiry to the touch, and the fronds are long slender filaments. Unlike the **Sea Lettuce** and **Sea Grass** (*Ulva* spp), it has a deep green colouration. It reproduces during the Summer months, but I have not seen its reproductive structures which may be microscopic. Common Green Branched Weed is relatively common at Ross and is sporadically found throughout the Irish coastline and elsewhere.

Left:The fuzzy look of Common Green Branched Weed in April.

All year around - Bushy Rainbow Wrack
Cystoseira tamariscifolia

Bushy Rainbow Wrack

(1)**Bushy Rainbow Wrack** (*Cystoseira tamariscifolia*), laden with an unknown epiphytic seaweed(2) in a middle shore rock pool at Ross, in mid March.

Found in just a small number of relatively deep middle shore pools at Ross, the true beauty of **Bushy Rainbow Wrack** can really only be appreciated from underwater. At surface level, its iridescence is un-noticeable, presenting as a straggly, exceptionally bushy plant that lingers close to the surface of the pool being buoyed by a few small air bladders. However, this changes, when one captures it from below the surface. This seaweed, which is a hermaphrodite, has a westernly and southern distribution around the Irish and British coast where it can form 'bushy forests' in rockpools together with other members of the *Cystoseira* (Bushy Wracks) family.

All year around - Japanese Wireweed (*Sargassum muticum*)

Invasive

Japanese Wireweed (*Sargassum muticum*), has steadily crept into the shoreline habitats at Ross beach without much attention. Our research of the beach commenced in 2009. It was Spring 2011, before James and I noticed the first specimen of Japanese Wireweed in a rockpool to the western side of the beach. We have been astounded with its continuous spread on the beach since then. This is a distinctive brown seaweed with small stalked air bladders as seen in (1). In deeper rock pools, small plants can be seen in a vertical position, buoyed by the myriad of air bladders as seen in (2). It is bushy, with abundant branchlets containing small oval shaped fronds with irregular edges.

This rapidly growing invasive seaweed was first recorded in British waters in the 1970s. Growing up to 7cm per day, in warm temperate conditions, it has spread rapidly around the British and Irish coastline. It is considered a nuisance at the entrance to harbours, and can easily out compete native species by virtue of the fact that it grows so rapidly, reproduces quickly and if broken up can regenerate from both ends of itself.

During the warm Summer of 2013, large swathes of the seaweed, could be found forming a canopy in the shallow sub-tidal at Ross, just beyond the stretch of Thong Weed (*Himanthalia elongata*) as seen at (3). Over the ensuing stormy winter, large batches of kelps and shore seaweeds have been driven off shore. It will be interesting to note the impact of these extreme conditions on the population of Wireweed during the upcoming Summer of 2014. I have captured images of this seaweed from middle shore rock pools in March 2014.

In the book '**Irish Seaweed Kitchen**' by Dr. Prannie Rhatigan, *Sargassum* is described as an edible seaweed, with a balanced range of nutrients and a relatively high mineral content, especially magnesium.

All year around - Corallinaceae Crusts
(Lithophyllum & Lithothamnion)

Corallinaceae Crusts are encrusting and crustose seaweeds, that sheath large surface areas of rocks, boulders, basins of rock pools and foliose seaweeds from the upper shore level down to the shallow sub-tidal. They are hardened calcified seaweeds that do not easily lend themselves to grazers like Limpets (*Patella sp.*) and Periwinkles (*Littorina sp.*). Limpets seen grazing atop these seaweeds, are generally grazing a biomass film that lingers over the calcified seaweeds. This is actually providing a valuable service to the encrusting seaweed, ensuring its surface remains free to photosynthesize and not become overgrown with other seaweeds.

Corallinaceae crusts vary in colour, shape, texture and pattern. At the top of the shore in shallow well lit pools or on open, always wet rock surfaces one finds pale pink, almost smooth paint like seaweed. This is most likely to be **Overgrowing Paint Weed** (*Lithothamnion crouaniorum*). This covers large areas, hugs rock surface texture and offers a lovely colour variation on the shore. This seaweed can be seen right throughout the year. Some of these encrusting seaweeds grow to become thick and knobbly, while maintaining the same soft pink hue and occupying the same upper levels on the shore. These hardened, distinctly attractive textured varieties, which may appear like sponges, are most likely to be **Common Pale Paint Weed** (*Lithophyllum incrustans*). This specie can look spectacular in well lit, well diversified rock pools.

Studying the fronds of Carrigeen (*Chondrus chrispus, Mastocarpus stellatus*), and sometimes on the stipes of Forest Kelp (*Laminaria hyperborea*), one finds an epiphytic roughly textured, mid rose pink blobby seaweed, which will most likely be **Little Gem Paint Weed** (*Titanoderma pustulatum*).

Down on the lower shore, and especially hidden under large tracts of wracks like Serrated Wrack (*Fucus serratus*) and Egg Wrack (*Ascophyllum nosodum*), one finds encrusting seaweeds with a much deeper reddish/pink/purple hue. This deeper encrusting seaweed can also be found at the base of heavily occupied and shaded deep pools on the lower shore. Species of encrusting seaweeds at this level include **Common Shore Paint Weed** (*Phymatolithon lenormandii*), and **Common Purple Paint Weed** (*Phymatolithon purpureum*). Sometimes, with so little un-occupied rock surface space, these encrusting seaweeds appear as a 'coat' over limpet and periwinkle shells and can be most attractive. These seaweeds, which are slow growing and long lived require very little light to photosynthesize.

Higher up on the shore at Ross, typically in iron oxidized and well lit shale rock pools, one finds exquisite pattern-forming Brown encrusting seaweed. Set against the rustic colouration of the iron oxide, this attractive circular forming patchwork may be the crustose phase of a foliose seaweed. Limpets too, may be coated in an encrusting seaweed, known as **Brown Limpet Paint** (*Ralfsia verrucosa*)

Encrusting seaweeds do not take on any particular shape, but often have a 'rounded' appearance with almost frilly edges that are often tinged in white which is due to the high density of calcium carbonate at the edges.

Some encrusting species, are the beginning phase of foliose varieties. The Carrigeen (*Mastocarpus stellatus*), for instance falls into this category, where it may exist for up to 90 years as an encrusting paint seaweed before developing its distinctive foliose phase.

Such a variety, and so difficult to identify one from another. As shore spotters, however, having an insight to the variety and specific habitat of each encrusting seaweed, serves to raise the level of awareness and appreciation of the immense shore diversity. At Ross this diversity plays out over a small tract of shoreline, and low vertical gradient. This in itself is the magic, that caused me to research Ross beach like a starving fish monger, never leaving its shoreline unfulfilled.

Current economic use of Coralline algae include its use in medical science in dental bone implants. In Britain and France it has been used as a soil conditioner and has been sought after as an attractive and ecologically important component of fish tanks.

In a well lit, shallow, upper middle shore rock pool, a distinctive pale pink encrusting seaweed **Common Pale Paint Weed** (*Lithophyllum incrustans*)(1), provides a knobbly textured feature to a pool that is also occupied by colourful Anemones, Glass Prawns, Hermit Crabs, Calcareous Tube Worms and other inhabitants.

In a deep and shaded lower shore rockpool, thin and thicker varieties of a rich pink encrusting seaweed, perhaps **Common Shore Paint Weed** (*Phymatolithon lenormandii*) (1), share space, probably overgrown by encrusting forms of young foliose seaweeds. Young brown mid-ribbed plants of **Bladder Wrack** (*F. vesiculosus*) (2) can be seen emerging, as well as that of dark red **Carrigeen** (3). When combined with organic shell and pebble rubble, the pool provides for an interesting viewing.

On the lower shore, the floor of a shaded deep sandstone rock pool is almost completely lined in a coating of lower shore Coralline species, possibly **Common Purple Paint Weed** (*Phymatolithon purpureum*)(1). The well cemented claw-like holdfast of **Tangle Kelp** (*Laminaria digitata*)(2), and the insignificant **Common Green Branched Weed** (*Cladophora rupestris*)(3) also inhabit the pool, with grazing attempts made by *Littorina* and *Trochidae*(4)

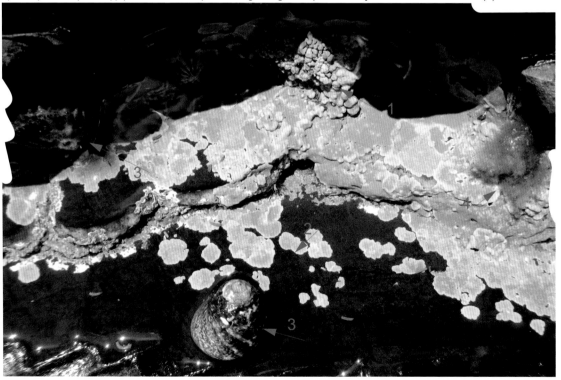

On a continuously wet, trickle flowing rock surface on the middle shore, an interesting assemblage unfolds. The textured, knobbly growth of the **Common Pale Paint Weed** (*Lithophyllum incrustans*)(1) is met by the delicate, flat patch-forming **Overgrowing Paint Weed** (*Lithothamnion crouaniorum*)(2). Grazers present include *Patella vulgata* and *Osilinus lineatus*(3) and seem to be avoiding the paint weeds, while an unidentified filamentous green seaweed, possibly *Cladophora spp.* adds delicate colour variation.

Nestling in an open sky facing shallow pool at the upper middle end of the shore, amongst interesting rock formations that are rustic coated by heavy concentrations of iron oxide, itself providing a handsome backdrop for the plate like pattern forming brown encrusting species(1). At this open location, seaweeds need to tolerate low salinity levels.

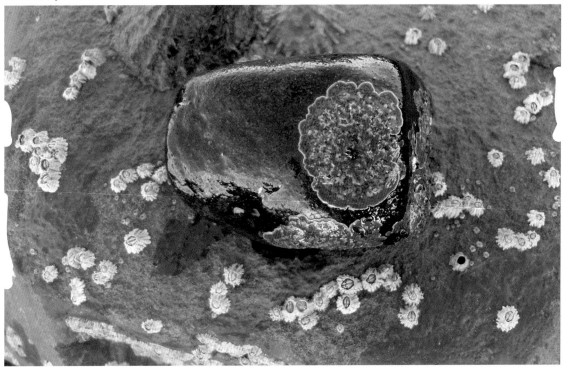

The real beauty of the irregular formations of red encrusting seaweeds can be viewed in this small encrusted boulder, depicting rounded frilly calcium carbonate tipped edges. It is important not to remove seaweed laden boulders like this from the shore as such seaweeds will not survive outside their particular habitat.

All year around - Bladder Wrack
Fucus vesiculosus

Bladder Wrack (*Fucus vesiculosus*) key features include paired circular air bladders(1) that flank either side of the very distinctive mid-rib(3). The fronds(4) are tough and leathery and vary in colour from light golden olive in Spring into Summer and dull dark brown during Winter. The female of the species bears large long/oval reproductive structures (2) at the tips of the fronds that should not be confused with the circular air bladders (1)which appear throughout the upper frond. I mostly find specimens with these in the Spring time.

Bladder Wrack(*Fucus vesiculosus*), is not overly abundant at Ross Beach, and where it does appear, it is normally located on the middle and lower shore. The Bladder Wrack is an easily identifiable much branched seaweed that attaches to rock and boulder via a well cemented disk-like holdfast. The air bladders are smooth, rounded and paired, and the mid-rib is very distinctive. The Frond is leathery and wavy edged. Colonies of calcareous Tube Worms (*Spirobis spp*), can be seen on the fronds from time to time. According to Dr. Prannie Rhatigan's book '**Irish Seaweed Kitchen**', this is an edible seaweed. It is found on both sides of the Atlantic and in the Baltic Sea and it is used worldwide in the cosmetics industry on a significant quantity of upmarket, gels, creams, anti-cellulite and anti-ageing products. It is also used as nutrition and diet supplements for people and animals.

All year around - Discoid Fork Weed
Polyides rotundus

Discoid Fork Weed (*Polyides rotundus*)(1) is a normally upright growing, distinctive red seaweed. It has fleshy rounded fronds, which are circular in cross section. Discoid Fork Weed plays host to several species including the **Purse Sponge** lookalike colonial **Sea Squirts** *(Didemnid sp)*(2), which wrap around the slender fronds, in the process finding themselves a long term home.

Clawed Fork Weed(*Furellaria lumbricalis*) - above with male reproductive structures.

Discoid Fork Weed (*Polyides rotundus*), is an attractive plant that thrives in the gravelly shallow sub-tidal at Ross Beach with its discoid holdfast buried in the gravelly sediment. In this habitat, it is quite abundant, looking its best in early Summer when new growth and light resurrects it from its dull winter colour which is likely to be a dull brown. This seaweed is distinctive, often heavily clad in the **Purse Sponge**, which also thrives in this particular habitat, and in an encrusting epiphytic seaweed, probably **Little Gem Paint Weed** (*Titanoderma pustulatum*). Discoid Fork Weed may be easily confused with a similar species **Clawed Fork Weed** (*Furcellaria lumbricalis*) (3), Clawed Fork Weed, like the Discoid Fork Weed have male and female specimens with the male plants showing distinctive swellings (4), when in reproductive mode, in early Spring. Clawed Fork Weed has a brownish colour when held up to light, and tends to be bigger and less tidy than Discoid Fork Weed.

All year around - Common Coral Weed
Corallina officinalis

Common Coral Weed (*Corallina officinalis*) is a small bushy pink seaweed, that is rarely grazed by gastropods such as Limpets (*Patella*) and Periwinkles *(Littorina)* due to its hard calcified constituency.

This is one foliose seaweed that grows from a basal crust as seen in (2)

One of the most distinctive and easily recognised seaweeds on the shore, the **Common Coral Weed**, (*Corallina officinalis*)(1)presents abundantly throughout the shore, from middle shore rock pools attached to the bedrock, to deeper lower shore pools and into the shallow sub-tidal. This seaweed can often look its best during the Winter months and into the Spring, as strong sun in Summer can bleach it white and whither it. This seaweed often grows as a rim around rockpools. It is a stiff calcified seaweed that is closely related to the encrusting paint forms. The seaweed itself has a segmented stipe, and a much divided branching system. This segmentation allows the seaweed to move with flexibility in the water column. The tips are often a white colour and this is because it contains a greater density of calcium carbonate at the tips. Coral weed is attractive and abundant and there are 'fields' of it at Ross. From a reproduction standpoint, each specimen is either male or female. Corallina algae is an important ingredient in the cosmetics industry and is used across a wide range of products.

All year around - Pink Plates Seaweed
Mesophyllum lichenoides

Pink Plates
(*Mesophyllum lichenoides*)

There are dense turfs of **Coral Weed** occuping rock shelves on the extreme lower shore at Ross. It's in these fields of pink that I find the hemispherical and circular forming plate-like seaweed, known as **Pink Plates** (*Mesophyllum lichenoides*). This seaweed only grows on Coral Weed, therefore it is an epiphyte. This is a hard calcified seaweed, that forms layers of plates and it is common at this particular site. Its surface may host protruding white circular spots. These are the reproductive spores. The seaweed has male and female individuals and both sexes hold spores which are eventually shed through openings at the top of the spores. The seaweed also hosts concentric rings, possibly growth rings. This seaweed occurs frequently around the southern and western coasts of Ireland, parts of eastern Scotland and south west Britain.

All year around - Brown Tuning Fork Weed
Bifurcaria bifurcata

All year around - Codium
Codium fragile

According to the Seasearch distribution map (2010), **Brown Tuning Fork Weed** (*Bifurcaria bifurcata*)(1), has quite a limited distribution in the British Isles, with distributions limited to the southern English Coast, Channel Islands, the northern coast of Donegal, Sligo, Galway Bay, parts of the Clare coast and south west Cork. At Ross beach it is present in just a couple of deeper pools at the mid shore level. These pools are also heavily occupied with the bushy wracks (*Cystoseira spp.*), **Wireweed** (*Sargassum*) and others. This distinctive seaweed, ranges in colour from light green to golden and has much branched circular fronds. Each specimen contains both male and female structures.

A very distinctive dark green species, **Codium** (*Codium fragile*) (2) has a floppy spongy texture, but when appearing in rock pools, mostly shallow pools on the middle shore, it is upright, being buoyed by its hollow spongy structure. It is not common here and tends to be much smaller than the washed up specimen at (2). According to Prannie Rhatigan's book 'Irish Seaweed Kitchen', this is an edible species.

Mother's Day

Like a message in a bottle, the message from this shallow sub-tidal heart shaped, beautiful pink paint encrusted rock, seemed to read ' **Happy Mother's Day**' as I wander, head bowed, through the subtidal in the glistening sunshine on Mother's Day 2014. A pretty little seaweed habitat from the broken shell and sand scoured sea bed. The Straggly brown seaweed at the top is probably '*Ahnfeltia plicata*.'

Fleshy red species
Red Rags
(*Dilsea carnosa*)

Frequently found throughout the year in the shallow sub-tidal at Ross. **Red Rags** always appears to be torn, broken or partially eaten. I can see why this seaweed may receive a common name 'Red Rags'.

Depending on the quantity of light shining through the sub-tidal, together with coverage from higher layers such as Sugar Kelp, one can encounter Red Rags in a wide variety of hues. It is at its brightest when exposed to direct light. In Winter time, this broad fronded, seaweed may appear a very dull maroon red. It has a small discoid holdfast, and there are male and female individuals with reproduction taking place during the Winter months.

As a seaweed it has a much thicker consistency than that of all other red species. It doesn't have a mid-rib, and would be viewed as a robust flat red species. The edible red species **Dillisk** - *Palmata palmaria* would also be classed in the same category. However, Red Rags is not an edible seaweed.

Red Rags is distributed around the coast of Ireland, Britain, the Nordic Countries, and south to Portugal.

Red Rags

Tapering Frond

Fleshy

All year around - Delicate Species
Banded Pincer Weeds
Ceramium spp.

To truly appreciate this delicate brown tufted seaweed, it needs to be studied close up. Its axes are cylindrical and banded and its tips have a pincer-like formation.

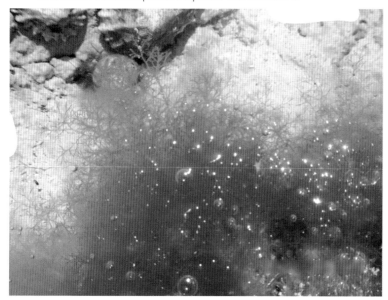

In a typical middle shore rock pool in the height of Summer, **Banded Pincer Weed** forms part of the mix, offering delicacy and a golden hue, which combined with Pink Paint Seaweed, Punctured Ball Weed, Limpets, Periwinkles, Topshells, Glass Prawns and others provides enough viewing to lose the day here.

Delicate, fibrous, branching, **Banded Pincer Weeds** (*Ceramium spp.*) need to be seen up close to be appreciated. Banded Pincer Weeds are common at Ross, and even though approximately fourteen species can be found in Irish and British coastal waters, I am happy to view them as an overall group. Awarding individual identifications within this grouping is beyond the scope of this book. Banded Pincer Weeds are to be found, throughout the year. In well lit middle shore rock pools in Summer, they appear golden and delicate to a sewing thread, bushy, much branched and it becomes difficult to capture their true beauty and characteristics on camera. Finding species in the shallow sub-tidal throughout the year, they are often darker, sprawling, longer and slightly wiry to touch.

All year around - Pool Living Red Species

Deep Lower Shore Pool

Occupying deeper pools on the middle and lower shore throughout the year, but looking their best during late Spring into Summer, these medium sized branching reds add alot of colour to their habitat. The image above, has posed alot of difficulty with its identification and indeed image making, but it is common here and I believe it to be a member of the **Siphoned Weed** family (*Polysiphonia spp.*).

Less common, is the **Branched Wing Weed** (*Pterocladia capillacea*)(left), and it is often encountered intermingled with the **Bushy Wracks** and **Brown Tuning Fork Weed** of deep middle shore pools.

All year around - Delicate Species
Cocks Comb *Plocamium spp.*

One of the most attractive and abundant species of the shore by virtue of its extensive delicate detailing, **Cock's Comb** (*Plocamium spp.*) is part of a grouping of four distinct species. During Winter months, it is a dull dark red colour, and one has to temporarily remove it, to examine its identity. At this time it can also be festooned with Coralline algae and Bryozoans.

During Summer months, it can appear a very bright red or orange, having being bleached by the sun.

This seaweed can be encountered in shore rock pools, free floating in the shallow sub-tidal, attached to bed rock and growing on the stipes of Forest Kelp (*Laminata hyperborea*).

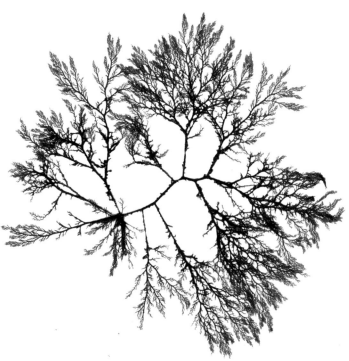

Beautiful Fan Weed *Callophyllis laciniata.*

Wading through the shallow sub-tida during the Summer months, one is met with more red species than at any other time of year. At this time the abundance of **Beautiful Fan Weed** (*Callophyllis laciniata*) is apparent. In the inner sub-tidal, it free-floats with abundance, merged with other species in a multi-storey co-habitation. I believe this specie is present to some degree all year around, often looking dull and dark red during Winter or taking on a more insipid orange red hue on occasion. This is a flat fronded fan shaped seaweed with lovely irregular detailing at the frond tips. This seaweed normally grows on the stipes of Forest Kelp and is a characteristic plant of this habitat. The plants that I encounter are detached specimens.

The Kelp Forest & its year around species

Kelp Forest

Perhaps the most commonly viewed seaweeds on any given beach are those which are landed in vast quantities on the shore. The main component of this beached seaweed cache are the significantly sized Kelps. These are the largest seaweeds, forming a category of their own and all are brown seaweed species. These are very important ecological seaweeds, providing, shelter, home, food and surface on which to deposit the eggs of several species of sea slugs. In addition, these seaweeds, which survive in the direct line of ocean movements, have a certain level of ability to tame incoming water movement as it nears the shoreline. In addition many of these seaweeds have commercially sought properties and indeed have been collected at this shore for many decades, maybe generations. The density and variety of the kelps growing free standing from the substratum just on the fringe of the shallow sub-tidal at low spring tide, and out to sea, is known as the Kelp Forest. Species such as **Forest Kelp** (*Laminaria hyperborea*), have stout, stiff rounded stipes (stems), which are often referred to as 'Sea Rods'. These are distinctive among landed species on the beach. Other seaweeds such as **Tangle Kelp** (*Laminaria digitata),* have flexible rounded stipes, which allow the seaweed to move easily with the water flow. As Ross is a north west facing beach on the Atlantic coastline, it is particularly prone to northerly storms, which, when combined with a spring tide can reek havoc on the natural distributions and populations on the beach together with its boundary and surrounding lands. This is the time that Kelps are most at risk here, and with them all their sheltered creatures and epiphytic seaweeds. Kelps, especially, Forest Kelp is known to host up to two hundred living organisms, all of whom play a part in the food chain. Serious loss of the Kelp Forest during ocean storms is therefore the death knell for millions of living creatures and plants every time.

All year around - Kelp Forest Species
Forest Kelp - *Laminaria hyperborea*

Forest Kelp (*Laminaria hyperborea*)(1), stipes and large digit fronds washed up at Ross. This biomass can be brought ashore at any time of year, when the ocean is turbulent and when there are strong northerly ocean storms. Up to and including the time of World War 11, these locally named 'Sea Rods' were collected here, formed into bales and sold on to agents. These '**Sea Rods**' have many uses, in cosmetics, agriculture and in medicine. As with all Kelps, Forest Kelp is rich in iodine. During harvest time, various Kelps were collected - especially the more easily accessible **Sugar Kelp** (*Saccharina latissima*), dried and then burnt in stone clad kiln drains - a process that lasted several days, before the burnt remains were bagged and sold to agents for further processing into various products. Various research has been carried out into the potential for mechanical Kelp harvesting off the Irish coastline. However, no mechanical Kelp harvesting occurs at this time.

A close study of the claw-like holdfast and stipe of Forest Kelp (2) reveals a myriad of tiny creatures, young life, ribbon eggs, epiphytic seaweeds of the encrusting and red foliose variety.

In addition, a cross sectioning of the stipe reveals concentric annual growth rings, akin to those of a tree. If undisturbed, it is known to have a long lifespan 10-20 years, much longer than that of the other Kelps. Peak annual growth happens during Winter from January to June and growth stops over the Summer period.

Forest Kelp is a north east Atlantic species, that thrives from Scandanavia to the Canaries. It is commercially harvested in some countries, especially Norway and Iceland. Norway harvests c.160,000t pa. It has uses right across several industries from bio-technology to food processing, medical, cosmetic and agricultural.

Forest Kelp is therefore a seaweed of immense ecological and commercial importance. Yet so much beached Kelp remains wasted and left to decay on the shoreline. Yes, these nutrients will find their way down shore again, but perhaps, it is time to reconsider sustainable harvesting or ad hoc collection of this important resource on a small scale for high end, high value products.

According to the Seaweed Industry Association, a study of Forest Kelp showed that in one plant 238 species were located numbering 8000 individuals. A closer look at the clawed holdfast (left) reveals a tiny bivalve beginning its life here. Unfortunately it is only as secure as its host. This landed specimen, which has been completely uprooted, during an ocean storm, signifies a definite end to its young life.

All year around - Kelp Forest Species
Furbellows Kelp (*Saccorhiza polyschides*)

Meeting a fully in tact, fully grown free floating, **Furbellows Kelp** (*Saccorhiza polyschides*)(1) during one of my Summer Rocky Shore Field Tours was greeted with gasps of sheer astonishment by my audience. They had never viewed such a wonderfully textured, large - to three metres tall seaweed before. This is a specie from the Kelp Forest, generally beyond the reach of normal shore walkers. It is exquisitely crafted, with a significant, circular forming, densely warty and hollow holdfast. This holdfast normally attaches to a stable substrata, but as aforementioned, unlike land plants, it does not draw in nutrients from its under surface via this holding mechanism, so when encountered free floating in the water, it is very much alive and photosynthesizing. The problem arises when it is beached out of water. It cannot live out of water, so dessication sets in quickly. Above the warty holdfast, the stipe base consists of a pattern forming frilly growth formation, narrowing into a stiff leathery strap like stipe, a sort of basal re-enforcement, and allowing for greater flexibility in continuous water movement. The fronds are long and untidy digits measuring up to a metre long.

The Furbellows Kelp is by no means as abundant as the Forest Kelp, with which it shares its habitat at Ross. On assessing beached biomass after storms, it is much more common to encounter Tangle Kelp (*Laminaria digitata*), Sugar Kelp (*Saccharina latissima)* and Forest Kelp (*Laminaria hyperborea*), than the odd specimen of Furbellows (*Saccorhiza polyschides*)(2). Furbellows Kelp is a rapid colonizer of cleared areas, is a short lived and fast growing species, typically living less than one year. Reproduction takes place between October and May.

All year around - Kelp Forest Species
Tangle Kelp (*Laminaria digitata*)

A densely covered boulder on the extreme lower shore in early Summer, provides clues to the wonderful variety, colour, texture and abundance of free growing wild seaweeds at Ross.

Another member of the Kelp Forest, and flanking the in shore fringes of the forest, **Tangle Kelp** (*Laminaria digitata*)(1)may also have individual specimens located in lower shore pools and on the extreme lower shore exposed at low Spring tides. This is another large Kelp, to 1.5 metres, consisting of a small claw-like holdfast, generally a short flexible oval stipe (2) and smooth evenly divided frond segments that are tough and leathery. Unlike the rod-like stipe of the Forest Kelp, the stipe of Tangle kelp flops over when out of water. This kelp may bear some resemblence to another brown seaweed - **Broad Leaf Weed** (*Petalonia fascia*), also found at Ross, but this is generally smaller and generally has two thin fronds, one of which is a very wide sheath.

Tangle Kelp has a complicated reproduction process, that consists of two phases, the second phase generating the large Kelp. Reproduction occurs during Summer months and growth commences from Autumn continuing through Winter. Tangle Kelp has been the subject of much commercial Aqua culture research and has extensive valuable properties. It is currently harvested, dried, packaged from wild stocks by the Wild Irish Sea Vegetable Company for the Irish and export markets.

While it would not have been part of our local coastal tradition to eat this particular seaweed, Dr. Prannie Rhatigan's book 'Irish Seaweed Kitchen' provides mouth watering recipes, and simple suggestions like wrapping the fronds around white fish before baking the fish.

Kelp Forest Species
Sugar Kelp (*Saccharina latissima*)

The claw-like cemented holdfasts of **Sugar Kelp** look spectacular in this late April picture, taken during low spring tide. Sugar Kelp can tolerate periods out of water. In Summer its broad textured frond becomes a host for a myriad of tiny creatures, including **Coiled Tube Worms** (*Spirobis* spp) and **Star Ascidians** (*Botryllus schlosseri*).

One of my favourite species at Ross Beach, and highly abundant here, the frilly edged, broad fronded, wave textured surface of the **Sugar Kelp** (*Saccharina latissima*)(1), grows very rapidly from any suitable substratum including small rocks located in the inner fringe of the shallow sub-tidal. The outward stretch is unknown to me, but judging by the vast quantity of the species that arrives onshore at the end of the Autumn or during ocean turbulence, it most likely occupies a broad area of suitable habitat. This is an annual species, that easily detaches with a poor holding claw like holdfast(2). Both the holdfast and stipe are similar to that of Tangle Kelp (*Laminaria digitata*).

It often occurs to me, when walking and studying the shoreline, how difficult it becomes to make generalizations about any particular species. Albeit the fact that this is an annual species commencing growth in Spring, it is entirely possible to find toughened much darker specimens growing and commencing growth throughout the Winter months. Its fronds provide the surface of choice for a selection of sea slug eggs in springtime.

Kelp Forest Species
Sugar Kelp (*Saccharina latissima*)

During Autumn, huge drifts of **Sugar Kelp**, float in and out with the tide as it slowly decays at the end of its season, filtering nutrients back into the ocean. Eventually, turbulent seas will drive it beyond the normal tidal range, and it will become a feeding ground for **Kelp Flies** (*Coelopa frigida*) and coastal birds.

In early Summer, the young Sugar Kelp can have a tender texture and a light golden hue. Its growth season can commence as early as January.

During the Summer months, the **Snakelocks Anemone** (*Anemonia viridis*), attaches itself to the upper surfaces of the fronds of Sugar Kelp. The Snakelocks needs light to feed its symbiotic algae, which forms the green and purple tips on the tentacles of this species. I have yet to discover a Snakelocks being beached with the Kelp in the Autumn, and I believe that at some point they detach themselves from the Kelp and I find them occupying more benthic locations during the Winter months.

Sugar Kelp is an edible and commercially harvested seaweed. The Wild Irish Sea Vegetable Company based at Spanish Point, Co. Clare, sustainably hand pick, Sugar Kelp, dry it and package it for home and export markets. As a Kelp it is specifically high in iodine, but is also a rich source of calcium and iron together with many other trace minerals and vitamins. It can be eaten direct or experimented with in cooking. Prannie Rhatigan's 'Irish Seaweed Kitchen', provides interesting 'sweet' recipes using this seaweed.

As an artist, I have been so taken with its surface texture, that I have preserved it in textured artworks, where it looks like the surface of the ocean itself.

During Spring, very visible and rapid changes occur on the shore. It is a time of new growth, regeneration of dormant species, and an important time for reproduction of shore fauna.

Part of my interest in researching this book was to look for some visual semblances of change throughout the seasons on the rocky shore. This was something that didn't appear well documented on any informational resource that I had available. When I went searching for seasonal variation, I found it in abundance, both visibly and subtly. Reading the shoreline through its seasonal variations brought a whole new wondrous dimension to each shore visit.

The seaweeds that I have described so far in this book are likely to be encountered right throughout the year at Ross. Some, like the Sugar Kelp will not be at its best in mid-Winter, but it will be present nonetheless. Some seaweeds that appear in the next section are actually described as 'Winter' seaweeds, but really their main growth in normal conditions may commence as early as December and they will have reached their full growth and be at their best during the Spring. My focus is on seaweeds, that are visibly spurting growth and achieving their full growth potential during these early months of the year. Seaweeds can grow quite rapidly, commence growth earlier than land plants, so long as favourable ocean conditions prevail. It's a wonderful time to visit the shore. Seaweeds are probably one of the most secretive hidden visions in our landscape/shorescape, yet provide a myriad of wonderful forms, colours, textures, and are choosey about their habitat. Seaweed spotting for the purposes of researching this book, has never failed to inspire me, confuse me and over-whelm me. It has taken close onshore monitoring, developing insights and understanding micro habitats, reading connections and consumers alike, through each Season over several years to get to this point which I present herewith.

Sea Grass (*Ulva compressa*)

Mid-March heralds a very visible transformation.

In time for St. Patrick's Day, the Limpets (*Patella spp.*) at the edge of the water at the front of the shore receive a green coating by mid March.

It is well into mid-Spring growth by March, for many shore line and shallow sub-tidal species. However, one of the most visible transformations of the entire year occurs from mid March, with the 'greening' of the lower shore shingle. This is **Sea Grass** (*Ulva* spp.)This shingle has been grey and bare over the Winter months, and its initial smooth coating on the smooth surfaces of the lower shore shingle is particularly beautiful. It is band-forming and appears in many of the seascape photos in this book. An exceptionally slippery seaweed though and one needs to thread through this narrow band of shingle at the entrance to the extreme lower shore and shallow sub-tidal with caution. It also graces the outer shells of Limpets (*Patella*) and can also be found in the shallow sub-tidal in gravelly patches. This coating develops into a foliose tube-like seaweed and can be found dangling off rock and boulder as Summer progresses. It eventually darkens into a deep green colour before losing its fronds leaving brown patches behind on the shingle. Shingle is not the preferred habitat of many species, because of its smoothness and lack of holding power together with the fact that shingle is at the outer rim of the water and remains out of water for much of the day. This is an edible seaweed closely related to Sea Lettuce (*Ulva lactuca*).

The semi-transparent blades of the edible Sea Lettuce provide a Spring green colour richness to the shore.

Looking down at the benthic species in the shallow sub-tidal during late April, one discovers an array of seaweeds reaching their prime for the season including the fully grown Sea Lettuce (*Ulva lactuca*).

The broad smooth blade forming **Sea Lettuce** (*Ulva lactuca*) commences growth as early as mid January and certainly by early February, there are many small semblances of this attractive seaweed to be found amongst gravel in shallow pools, attached to rock in shallow and deep pools and throughout the lower shore and shallow sub-tidal. This is a common seaweed at Ross, and like its land plant equivalent, is an edible seaweed, one of the most balanced nutritionally. This seaweed is rich in protein, vitamin C, iron, calcium, magnesium, iodine and a host of trace minerals and vitamins. James and I regularly eat some while on the shore. We are both in agreement that it has a delicate salty flavour. It is very suitable for salads and omelettes, and best used fresh. This seaweed lends itself to commercial harvesting for the fresh foods market and Gourmet dining and food outlets.

By late April, Sea Lettuce has fully grown and is exceptionally beautiful when seen through filtered light. It has developed broad smooth wavy edge fronds that splay across the pool or shallow subtidal.

Spring Species
Sliocháin (*Porphyra* spp.)

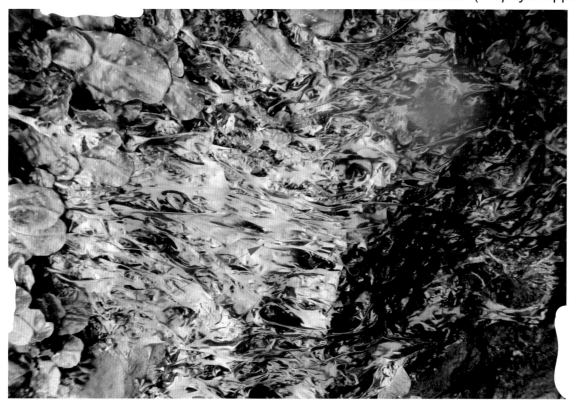

This dark red seaweed is known worldwide as **Nori** or **Laver**, but in Ireland and certainly West Clare it is known as **Sliocháin**. This seaweed is the most commercially harvested and economically valuable seaweed in the world. Nori is actively harvested via aqua-culture in Japan and Korea. This seaweed is harvested for the food industry and is often found as the wraparound sheets served in sushi dishes.

Back home at Ross, Loophead, **Sliocháin** is strongly associated with our community heritage and traditional food. Within our own immediate family, through all the generations that we can account for, Sliocáin was sought and actively harvested from wild stocks from December to March. It was closely monitored to ensure it was picked at the earliest possible moment. A Sliocháin meal was a celebratory meal, a celebration of something wild and only temporarily available. The time of harvest varies from one year to another and is dependent on elements such as frost tenderizing it for consumption. Harvesting this seaweed in our area is dangerous as the main crop is located off wave exposed vertical coast at Ross. Its appearance at Ross beach is entirely incidental and has given me the opportunity to write about such a precious seaweed.

Sliocháin is washed and traditionally cooked with bacon, making an utterly delicious mouth-watering meal during early Spring. It also lends itself to freezing and is often available to purchase from the local butcher when in Season. As a coastal native, I am not sure to what degree this traditional dish has penetrated inland, but my guess is that it remains a best kept secret of our coastal communities. This seaweed lends itself to commercial harvesting, and it is an exceptional high quality nutritious food that also cleanses the digestive system.

Like so many other seaweeds, Nori has a two phase life cycle, the first one is a microscopic one that encrusts on shells. It was an English botanist, Kathleen Drew Baker, that discovered this shell living first phase of the life-cycle of Nori. This information provided the Japanese with the knowledge they required to commercially grow and harvest Nori. Nori is now a 1.5bn dollar industry in Japan, making Nori (Sliocháin) the most valuable seaweed currently commercially harvested in the world.

Spring Species
Bunny-eared Bead Weed (*Lomentaria articulata*)

Although some traces of **Bunny-eared Bead Weed** (*Lomentaria articulata*) (1), can be found throughout the seasons, it is from early Spring that this juicy, beady, red seaweed begins to proliferate and add colour to the shoreline. It can be found across a number of habitats: dangling off shaded boulders, free-floating in the shallow sub-tidal, sometimes on lower shore rock pools. It grows to approx 10cms. It is very common here. The distinctive seaweed is normally attached to rock by a small discoid holdfast. It is heavily segmented into hollow 'beads' and it has a coral pinkish to red colouring. During the Summer months I encounter it free floating in the shallow sub-tidal. There are male and female specimens of the plant, and the male has paler beaded segments towards the tips of the seaweed. This seaweed is widely distributed around the Irish coastline.

A mid Summer seaweed assemblage demonstrates the form, diversity and colour available in a small space.

Pepper Dulse (*Osmundea pinnatifida*)

Often forming tufted patches on damp rock surface surrounding rock pools and stretching down into the extreme lower shore boulders, Pepper Dulse (*Osmundea pinnatifida*), is a Winter into early Summer seaweed that dies back over the Summer months, although one can still see its decayed remnants during this time. It attaches to rock via a tangled creeping holdfast. This is a small red seaweed species that grows to approx 8 cm. It is a member of a family of Flat Fern Weeds (*Osmundea* spp.) that can look alike and lead to identity confusion. This is an edible seaweed with a peppery smell.

This early March image (left) depicts the fern like short fronds of Pepper Dulse alongside the sprouting Bunny-eared Bead Weed from a heavily occupied rock surface on the lower shore. Both seaweeds can spend alot of time out of water, their preference being for exposed rock from the lower middle shore down.

Other Flat Fern Weeds (*Osmundea spp.*)

Also found at Ross Beach **Royal Fern Weed** (*Osmundea osmunda*) looks similiar to Pepper-Dulse, but there are a number of distinguishing features, the most obvious being the fact that it is a larger species growing up to 20cm in length. It also appears throughout the year, fringing rocks on the lower shore and in the shallow sub-tidal. Note the **Blue-rayed Limpet** (*Helcion pellucidum*) on the rock surface.

In the sunlit shallow sub-tidal in mid Summer, I am drawn to a reflection of another Fern Weed - either **Brittle Fern Weed** (*Osmundea oederi*) or **Rounded Brittle Fern Weed** (*Laurencia obtusa*) on the benthic floor. Both these species occupy similiar habitats and are normally submerged in rock pools or in the sub-tidal.

The stubby profile of **Brittle Fern Weed** (*Osmundea oederi*) in a middle shore rock pool in early Summer. I have not followed its growth pattern or its distribution enough to determine if it has a seasonal growth pattern. This seaweed is classed as a red seaweed, although it has a more golden hue.

I can never fail to be mesmerized by the intriguing beauty and growth pattern of **Thong Weed** (*Himanthalia elongata),* at Ross.

The variety of texture and colour provided by this combination of seaweeds in mid-Spring, provides for exquisite shore side seaweed spotting at this time.

By far one of the most distinctive and most common species of brown seaweed at Ross Beach, **Thong Weed** also known as **Sea Spagetti,** has a presence here all year round. However, during the Winter months it lays dormant in the form of pretty button like growths that are attached to rocky substratum by a discoid holdfast. The buttons are first tiny varying from 3mm to 1cm(1) before developing into a saucer-like shape with a central depression(2) out of which grows two long strap-like fronds(3). The fronds then further divide a number of times before reaching a maximum length by June of 2 to 3 metres. The pace of growth is rapid, and fully grown specimens can be found swirling on the surface of the water from late April. Although it doesn't have air bladders, the seaweed tends to stretch out toward the upper surface of the water. Thong weed is a significant feature of the shallow sub-tidal in the sheltered inner shore at Ross during the Summer months.

Spring Species
Thongweed (*Himanthalia elongata*)

This swirling pattern forming seaweed is an important and useful seaweed that is found along the north east Atlantic coastlines from the Baltic coast to Northern Spain and Portugal. It is rich in vitamins A, C & E along with amino acids and important minerals. It is incorporated as an ingredient in personal care products especially skin and scalp products, because of its skin protecting and nourishing properties. It is also an edible seaweed, that can be incorporated into sweet and savoury dishes. Dr. Prannie Rhatigan's book 'Irish Seaweed Kitchen' provides quite a variety of recipes for using fresh or dried Thong Weed. The Wild Irish Sea Vegetable Company harvests this seaweed for consumption and personal care products.

Thong Weed is an important ecological seaweed, providing itself as a host to epiphytic seaweeds. These are seaweeds that will commence their growth period during Mid Summer on the fully grown Thong Weed. The image on the right is taken in Mid-October, showing a fully developed epiphyte, possibly **Ceranium pedicellatum** (2)*,* growing on the outer edge of the frond. It is also frequented as a shelter by the **Blue-rayed Limpet** (*Helcion pellucidum*), who fits snugly beneath its narrow 1cm wide frond. The frond itself is tough and strap like and this is the harvestable part of the seaweed. Sustainable harvesting requires leaving approx one third of the frond behind, this will regenerate. The frond also contains the reproductive structures of the seaweed. Each individual is either male or female and the seaweed has a life span of two to five years.

During the late Autumn, the long fronds detach from the holdfast. This could be triggered by ocean turbulence. However it is a natural process. The image on the right was photographed in late October, it shows a twisting of the fronds. This may assist its detachment, and it may also be an outcome from its long persistence in the water for several months. Thong weed commences arriving on shore as early as the end of August, as early growing individuals reach maturity. Thong Weed forms part of the massive Autumnal biomass that arrives on shore at the end of its season, providing a wonderful opportunity for collection for fertilizing and conditioning nearby lands. My experience however, is that this cache is completely left to decay at its own natural destination, a missed opportunity for land users no doubt.

Spring Species
Punctured Ball Weed(*Leathesia difformis*)

The young Punctured Ball Weed (*Leathesia difformis*) in mid-March in a middle shore shallow pool.

Punctured Ball Weed has a two part life-cycle, and the other phase is that of a filamentous brown seaweed.

A most interesting shape and texture is added to the rocky shore at Ross, by the annual species **Punctured Ball Weed**(*Leathesia difformis*) that commences growth in early Spring, forming smooth globular formations in shallow middle shore pools, open middle shore rock surfaces and also heavily occupied rock surfaces in the extreme lower shore. As the season progresses, the globular form becomes irregular and hollow so that by late May, the rich golden coloured Punctured Ball Weed is somewhat colony forming and looking like that in the left image. In this assemblage it is sharing a heavily clad lower boulder with **Sea Lettuce** (*Ulva lactuca*), **Thong Weed** (*Himanthalia elongata*) and **Bunny-eared Bead Weed**(*Lomentaria articulata*). At this point in the season, they have all reached their peak and look healthy and splendid.

Spring Species
Oyster Thief(*Colpomenia peregrina*)

Another interesting Spring into Summer annual seaweed, **Oyster Thief** (*Calpomenia peregrina*) (1) can be found on lower shore rocks and free floating in the shallow sub-tidal right throughout the Summer months. Visitors on my Rocky Shore Field Trips are surprised to learn that this is actually a seaweed. The seaweed is hollow centred and papery to the touch and is an introduced species having come into British and Irish waters with shellfish movements. This species is common at Ross beach and is sporadically found around the Irish coastline.

Brown Wrack
Sea Oak(*Halidrys siliquosa*)

This large brown wrack seaweed is ever present but not exceptionally abundant, preferring a heavily disturbed exposed habitat. I often encounter the **Sea Oak** (*Halidrys siliquosa*) in free floating bunches in the shallow sub-tidal. It also frequents a few pools. It is a very flexible, but tough seaweed, and this flexibility is required for free movement in ocean currents. It can grow up to 120cm. The reproduction structures are bisexual and are found as bunches of stalked branched pods. The common name Sea Oak is also allocated to a red veined species, with no connections!

Spring into Summer Species

It is probable that many species have escaped my notice during the earlier part of Spring, being inconspicious by virtue of their tiny size at this time, while all the time I have been allowing myself be mesmerized by the spurting behaviour of the macro-algae. Indeed these are hard to escape, for everywhere their diversity of texture, colour, form and abundance is beckoning my attention.

During trips to the shallow sub-tidal from late April, one can be met with an array of brightly coloured, delicate species of seaweeds that are not present over the Winter months. These too seem fully grown by this time. One such spectacular seaweed is **Berry Wart Cress** (*Sphaerococcus coronopifolius*)(1). With late Spring light and sunshine this occasionally found free-floating species dazzles in a rustic orange-red hue. When viewed closely it has an opague appearance. Its main habitat is attachment to rock in the shallow sub-tidal.

Later in the Summer season, as uprooted 'Sea Rods' Forest Kelp (*Laminaria hyperborea*), drift inwards to the shore, a close examination yields amongst other organisms, an epiphytic feathery red seaweed **Feathered Wing Weed** (*Ptilota gunneri*)(2). This little weed is not present on Sea Rods arriving onshore during Winter months, and therefore it has either died down for the season or is not very abundant here.

Another extremely pretty, perfectly formed, delicate red seaweed found free floating in the shallow sub-tidal during Summer into Autumn months is the **Siphoned Feather Weed** (*Heterosiphonia plumosa*)(no image).

A sturdier red seaweed **False Eyelash Weed** (*Calliblepharis jubata*)(no image), is also found wandering freely in the shallow sub-tidal, close to shore. This is a much fringed species, and even though it has a full growth size of up to 30cm, the small number that I have found are much smaller. It can occur as an epiphyte attached to Coral Weed.

Summer Species
Fine-veined Crinkle Weed(*Cryptopleura ramosa*))

In the densely populated, magnificently diverse shallow sub-tidal at Ross during the Summer months, species of red seaweeds generally not encountered during the Winter months present themselves abundantly. Many are free- floating, perhaps detached from their host rock, plant, or animal. **Fine-veined Crinkle Weed** (*Cryptopleura ramosa*)(1), is widespread at this time and has a crinkled papery feel. This little veined species with spiraling fronds that have crinkled edges has a preference for the Kelp Forest, just beyond this region of the beach.

Another red seaweed featuring and looking its best at this time is the digit tipped, flat fronded **Great Rose Weed** (*Rhodophyllis* sp.)(2). This species is easily identified from other flat red seaweeds by a neat divided, rounded curving on its frond tips. This seaweed maybe present all year around.

Larger Veined Red Species

Found in a shallow middle shore pool, **Winged Weed** (*Membranaoptera alata*)(1), does not appear abundant here. Its preferred habitat is that of the lower shore, sub-tidal and Kelp Forest. This is an attractive red seaweed with long slender fronds, a mid-rib and visible lateral veins. The tip of the frond is divided and pincer-like. Maximum growth is approx 20cm. This is one seaweed that I have not encountered often or monitored its behaviour over a period of time.

In early Summer, encountering the broad fronded, wavy edged, mid-ribbed and veined **Sea Beech** (*Delesseria sanguinea*) (2) in a lower shore pool is a treat. Much later in the autumn, it loses its fronds with only the mid-rib remaining. As there are both male and female specimens of Sea Beech, they each produce reproductive structures on the naked mid-rib, with ferilization and reproduction taking place over the Winter months and new fronds growing in Spring.

Also occupying the pool is **Rounded Brittle Fern-weed** (*Laurencia obtusa*)(3), together with **Pink Paint Weed** (*Corallinaceae spp.*)

During early Autumn, in the midst of the biomass of end of season seaweeds lingering at the edge of the shore, one finds plenty samples of the tearaway look of **Sea Oak** (*Phycodrys rubens*)(4), quite often coated with the box-like patterns of Sea Mats. This too is a broad fronded, mid-ribbed and veined red seaweed. However its frond edges are lobed and serrated. This is a perennial seaweed that loses its leaf tissue during Winter leaving behind the mid-rib. This is a common seaweed in Irish and British coastal waters. Its perferred habitat is the sub-tidal, particularly the Kelp Forest and often attached to Forest Kelp (*Laminaria hyperborea*).

The wealth of beauty, colour, texture and abundance that I continually refer to in this book is very much evidenced in this mid July image, taken from the multi-layered shallow sub-tidal zone at Ross beach. Here seaweeds linger and peacefully co-exist like an entangled, carefree festival of the shore. All the time, ignored by terrestrial creatures, like us, too busy to celebrate the world with them. Beneath them, above them, attached to them, creatures like the Black Sea Cucumber, linger listless, the Snakelocks Anemone soaks in the Summer Sun and the baby Coiled Tube Worms, are happy to rest a top the holding texture of the Sugar Kelp.

It is in this environment that one finds **Divided Net Weed** (*Dictyota dichotoma*)(1), so different from the others, in an olive green hue with a lightweight papery texture, with bright mint green tips that lend themselves to some iridescence. With a pleasant notched and rounded tip, it is distinctive and abundant and mostly found free-floating in the shallow sub-tidal, before disappearing in the great Autumnal clearout.

Also in the image, **Sugar Kelp** (*Saccharina latissima*)(2), now in its fully grown tough leathery state and occupied by many shore fauna, the rounded frond and tips of **Discoid Fork Weed**(*Polyides rotundus*), abundant, attached and available right throughout the year, and the frilly, veined **Sea Oak** (*Phycodrys rubens*).

Summer in the middle and upper shore pools present a completely different array of flora and fauna. Indeed it is difficult to keep apace with continuously changing physical structures. A Summer species, a seaweed in reproduction flux, a physiological response to extremes of temperature, sunshine, rain. This is the drama that continually plays out on much more weather exposed upper and middle shore pools. The shallower the pool, the more the exposure from these elements.

Reading the pools is of course a source of great delight and entertainment. Peeping under boulders that may exist, will open up an often young world as newly born species are often safely tucked away here, until they grow and learn to cope with more turbulent exposures. Such under boulder inhabitants include the young **Flat Topshell** (*Gibbula umbilicalis*) and the young **Edible Periwinkle** (*Littorina littorea*), neither of whom receive parental care at any stage of their life-cycle.

Seaweeds vary from pool to pool. In the deeper pools there is normally a combination of the **Bushy Wracks, Brown Tuning Fork Weed, Codium,** and **Wireweed**. The combination of these bushy mid-sized weeds can appear like a miniature forest, and provides a sheltered habitat for many gastropod grazers, small fish and the Hermit Crab. In the shallow pools, species tend to be smaller and more delicate. In Pink Paint lined shallow pools one may find **Dumont Tubular Weed** (*Dumontia cortorta*) - not shown. This is a long stringy brown seaweed that is attached via a discoid holdfast. One will also find delicate 'Fuzzy' or thinly branched weeds, whose identity goes beyond the scope of this book. Also found are Brown Jelly Weeds most likely (*Eudesme virescens*)(1). The knobbly textured seaweed with filamentous hairs, is one form of the life-cycle of **Punctured Ball Weed** (2). Another common inhabitant of middle shore pools is **Maiden's Hair** (*Ectocarpus siliculosus*), a bushy and filamentous brown seaweed. Of course pools are also brimming with other year around species like **Carrigeen, Cocks Comb and Banded Pincer Weeds.**

Summer Species - in the Pools
Little Fat Sausage Weed
(*Champia parvula*)

Found in middle and upper middle shore pools during the Summer months, and perhaps lingering unnoticed during Winter months **Little Fat Sausage Weed** (*Champia parvula*), is juicy, fibrous, with blunted fronds that grow out at angles from the main axis.

The colouring varies from semi transparent to rose pink. I have located the seaweed in just a few pools and it is quite rarely found around the Irish and British coastline according to the Seasearch distribution Map (2010).

Summer Species
Desmarest's Flattened Weed(*Desmarestia ligulata*)

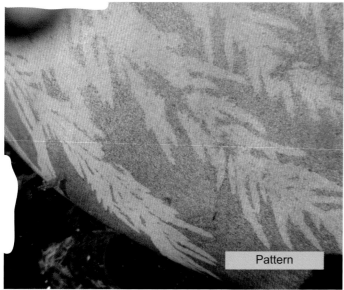

Pattern

During the sunny Summer of 2013, Desmarest's Flattened Weed had lingered atop this rock during part of a tidal cycle, in the process shading its image on to the rock. This is possibly due to its concentration of sulphuric acid, which burnt the biofilm.

Back on the shallow sub-tidal during Summer, **Desmarest's Flattened Weed,** (*Desmarestia ligulata*) another free floating specie has a preference for near surface occupation. This may be because it is flat and lightweight and buoyed by the water beneath. This is a large conspicuous much branched kelp species with a golden brown colouration. This species is meant to be attached to the substratum by a small bulbous holdfast, in the Kelp Forest. Being found freefloating, as aforementioned does not affect its ability to photosynthesize, which it does through its fronds. The overall seaweed has a ferny feel to it and it can grow to 2metres long.

This seaweed contains high concentrations of sulphuric acid, a great deterrent to grazers like Sea Urchins, whose five calcium carbonate teeth are actively dissolved by the seaweed, on grazing attempts. In this way it is also off-putting to seaweed grazing fish.

6 LIFE ABOVE THE TIDE-LINE

On the edge of the Atlantic ocean, in the narrow boundary between land and sea, just beyond the reach of the frequent tides (excepting Pulse Events), there lies a distinctive band of bedrock, salt marsh, shingle and clay providing the preferred habitat to a wide selection of terrestrial plants and coastal lichens. The portion of this area directly beyond the reach of the ocean is referred to as the 'splash zone'. It is the recipient of salty spray and salt laden winds and the community of organisms that eke out a living here have got to be salt and wind tolerant. Above that there is the Salt Marsh, always wet with withheld, ponding brackish water, laden with terrestrial plants like reeds and salt tolerant rush. Above that, and elevated, there are the soft margins, sometimes rocky margins of the edge of farmland facing onto the shore.

The 'Splash Zone' of Ross beach is dominated by bedrock containing a community of coastal lichens. The bedrock is a combination of formations from the ancient Namurian era, and consists mostly of sandstone, shale, slate and mud rock. Within this community species range from smooth paint like species like **Black Tar Lichen** (which does stretch down to the middle shore), to dense foliose varieties such as **Sea Ivory**. Lichens have been used since Victorian times as a barometer for clean air. They are easily killed by the presence of carbon monoxide and sulphur dioxide. Lichens are extremely slow growing, most species growing no more than a couple of millimeters pre year. With wide expanses of these lichens across our territory here they must be treated as an important part of our natural heritage - an ancient natural linkage.

Lichens are a composition of an algae and a fungus. These form a mutual symbiotic relationship, whereby the algae produces food through the process of photosynthesis and the fungus provides protection from the elements for the algae. Lichens are known to extend to the most exposed, harshest territories on the planet, being the only growth forms in exposed mountainous territory close to the extremities of the earth. They can withstand long periods of dessication, without water and with burning sun, by temporarily closing down their system, only to become active again, when the prevailing conditions are suitable. Lichens have been used, especially in Scotland, as a dye for wool. This was a significant industry around Glasgow, with thousands of people employed at one stage. It is still used to some extent in the Scottish islands as a dye. Lichens have other uses too. Lichens on rocky shore coastlines do stretch down below the splash zone, with particular species preferring to exist on the low and middle shoreline. So although these species do not fit into my Splash Zone community, I will nonetheless cover them in this section in an effort to present and compare the lichen heritage of Ross beach.

The Spash Zone at Ross is mainly composed of slumped and layered sandstone bedrock, with a relative smooth surface, intermingled with ponded channels. In the channels, one can find Gutweed growing at this level. **Gutweed** survives brackish water well, but wilts completely in continuous sunshine. It has an active reproductive agenda however, so it is constantly reproducing throughout the year. In crevices on the sandstone bedrock, one encounters singular plants of the deep rooted **Sea Thrift** (*Armeria maritima*), an exceptionally hardy plant, that doesn't survive within 200 metres of the coastline. At the edges of the higher ponds one meets a significant display of **Sea Milkwort** (*Glaux maritima*), another salt requiring plant that produces tiny pink flowers from May.

In the Summertime, the **Common Reed** is flush here in the salt marsh, providing a wonderful swaying sound with the constant warm breezes. It is intermingled with a significant density of **Sea Club Rush** *(Bolboschoenus maritima)*, and **Red Fescue** *(Festuca rubra)*. All these plants have deep, creeping roots that knit soil, providing an important function in holding soil, and stabilizing an otherwise unstable sandy/gravelly/muddy territory.

Facing onto the beach on the inner rim of the coastal ledge, is a muddy embankment, that is prone to attack by strong winds and turbulent oceans. The evidence of this is produced in scraws of knocked off vegetation hurled onto the sand and shingle. In the Summer there are patch forming clumps of **Wild Thyme** *(Thymus polytrichus)*, **Birds-foot Trefoil** *(Lotus corniculatus)*, **Kidney Vetch** *(Anthyllis vulneraria)*, **Wild Carrot** *(Daucus carota)*and **Sea Spurrey** *(Sperigularia rupicola)*, while at a lower level the sand is well covered with the **Creeping Silverweed** *(Potentilla anserina)* and the **Sea Mayweed** *(Tripleurospermum maritimum).* A complete list of flora is available in my book **'The Wild Flowers of Loophead'**. Little brown birds filter through this entire habitat, plucking worms and insects from the loose ground. My study does not extend to them at this point, but a very interesting book 'The Birds of Fanore' by John N. Murphy presents many of its likely inhabitants.

The slumped rock formation forming part of the splash zone at Ross Beach hosting a significant lichen community. Note the 'blackened' rocks is that of Black Tar Lichen (*Verrurcaria maura*)

Above the tide line but at the height of exposure from incoming ocean storms, a mixed territory of mud and rock, with patch forming flora on the muddy face, where they can set down roots, while a variety of encrusting and crustose lichens occupy the rock surface, not requiring mud or setting roots. There is evidence of coastal erosion here with newly broken off rock, leaving fresh surface space for succession to take place.

This highly serrated shale rock formation, generates a habitat that collects enough soil in its crevices for terrestrial plants to prosper alongside coastal lichens. Side by side with the sturdy **Sea Thrift** (*Armeria maritima*) there is the **Sea Plantain** (*Plantago maritima*), which also thrives here. The dominant lichens here are the **Sunburst Lichen**(*Xanthoria parietina*) and **Sea Ivory** (*Ramalina siliquosa*).

Lichen assemblage

At the top of the rocky shore, wild habitats continue to provide formation, textures, assemblages and exquisite beauty. The trick is to slow it down and open ones eyes to the finer detail, while all the time being dragged off focus by the bigger picture. In this assemblage, The **Black Shields Lichen** (*Lecanora atra*) provides the domination, it being the patch forming nobbly circular encrusting lichen with rimmed black fruiting bodies.

Upper Splash Zone - Lichen assemblage

Lichen assemblage

A beautiful textured and colourful assemblage formed on sandstone bedrock on the upper splash zone. To the front is the soft grey white crustose lichen *Ochrolechia parella*, with small turfs of an unidentifed black lichen together with specimens of the grey green foliose **Sea Ivory** and in the background the **Sunburst lichen**.

Sunburst Lichen (*Xanthoria parientina*)

For most species of coastal lichen, solid rock forms the most important substratum. Hard acid and rough surfaced rocks having the greatest variety of lichen species. Lichenologists, study the lichens of the seashore amongst other habitats. Their studies include zoning the splash zone and mid shore section of the shore into segments of rock type, surface, acidity and elevation level. For indeed, like the seaweeds of the shore, there are a number of environmental and habitat factors that determine, which specie is likely to grow and thrive on a particular rock.

At the higher levels of the splash zone, where the levels of salt spray declines, and bird droppings enrich the rock surface, the foliose **Sunburst lichen** (*Xanthoria parientina*) establishes itself as a main lichen specie. This lichen is not only a coastal lichen it can also be found inland. At Ross it forms dense coverage, adding its bright colour to this well lit shoreline. Its dominance arises to the eastern side of the beach, in relatively sheltered but well lit rock surfaces.

Upper Splash Zone - Lichen assemblage

Lichen coated landscape

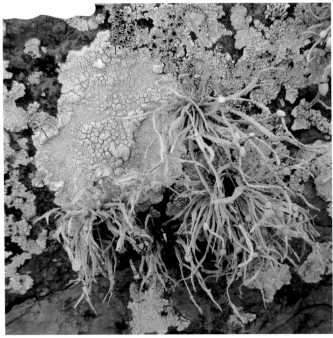

Perhaps one of the most visibly dominant lichen species of Ross beach is **Sea Ivory** (*Ramalina siliquosa*). It grows on seaward facing rocks, often mixed with other species including the **Black Shields** lichen, *Ochrolechia parella*, and **Sunburst lichen.** It has a rough, scruffy appearance, with strap like leaf structures that are grey green in colour. There are disk like fruiting bodies attached at the tip of this structure. These are the fruiting bodies of the fungus only. It is the name of the fungus that is used for the whole lichen, however, the fungus is not capable of free living. Each lichen consists of a different fungus, and only a certain few algae are capable of adapting by being incorporated into a fungus. The fungus occupies approx 90% of the lichen, and reproduction is normally by fungal spores that need to find a suitable algal partner or die. Sometimes lichens produce structures that contain both partners, which become detached and spread to new sites aided by wind, animals or rain.

Above and below the tide line - Lichen assemblage

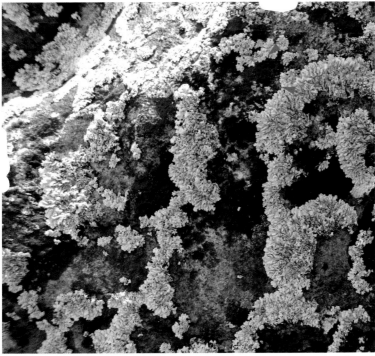

Black Tar Lichen (*Verrucaria maura*) and *Caloplaca spp.* are often found together.

Below the levels of Sea Ivory, Sunburst Lichen, and Black Shields Lichen, and being the recipients of alot more sea spray, sometimes ocean coverage are a congregation of Lichens that thrive in these conditions. Among these are the **Black Tar Lichen** (*Verrucaria maura*)(1), which extensively coats rock in a black paint like coverage. They often develop a chinky surface reminiscent of cracked dry mud, or produce low rounded bumps that protrude from the surface. Its choice of rock surface is limited to that of sandstone at Ross, where it offers no coverage to the shale, slate or mud stone present. Normally, sharing rock space at the upper limits is another yellow to orange specie, *Caloplaca spp.* This Lichen has a circular forming encrusting growth formation. When washed over by the odd rough Spring tide, it appears refreshed and a lighter yellow colour. There is a possibility that this same tide washes off some of the lichen leaving uncoated patches on the rock surface, as seen in the image. This is an attractive, pattern forming lichen, that prefers a sideline habitat, that is not directly in the oceans pathway.

Down at the mid shore level, in the midst of Barnacles and their predators, the Common Dog Whelk, another lichen forms widespread tufted patches, in well lit rock surface. This is the home of the **Black Tufted Lichen** (*Lichina pygmaea*), a nobbly, fruiticose lichen, which is associated with a tiny bivalve mollusc *Lasaea rubra*, which is only about 1mm in diameter. As a result, I have not, I'm afraid picked up this tiny free living creature during my research!

Looking closely at the tufted lichen, on the one hand it appears like Pepper Dulse seaweed gone off season, as its tufted structures bear a lobed like leaf structure. However, Pepper Dulse is found much lower down the shore. The bulbous fruiting bodies, which often appear green or yellow are distinctive. The Black Tufted Lichen grows on well lit sandstone rock with regular contributions of ocean coverage - twice daily.

Above and below the tide line - Lichen assemblage

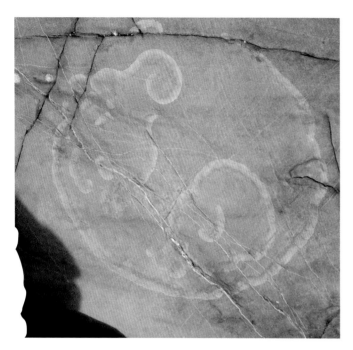

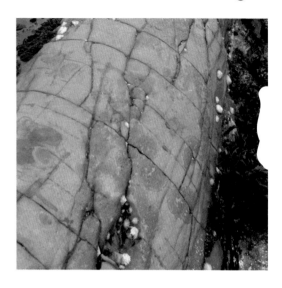

Moving downwards towards the lower shore and lower middle shore, another rock coating lichen becomes visible and dominant. This is another member of the 'Tar' (*Verrucaria* sp.) family. **Green Tar Lichen** (*Verrucaria mucosa*), forms circular patches and designs akin to cave art. On first encountering this lichen, it came to my attention by virtue of its art-like formation. It didn't occur to me that it was a lichen. With lichens growing so slowly, normally just a couple of millimetres per annum, the images I present herewith are indeed natures ancient living art.

Another fascinating discovery about this lichen is that it changes colour. I tried to observe a pattern for this, but none was forthcoming. Suffice to note, that on 1st of January 2012, on visiting Ross beach I am presented with the bright green image shown above left. This was an intriguing experience, as I had not noticed it green before. By the end of January 2012, it had darkened to a very dark black green, before returning to black and staying black for the rest of the year. I returned on New years day 2013, it was still black, but by early February it had turned to a mid green hue, lasting for a brief period before returning to black. I have been watching its movements ever since.

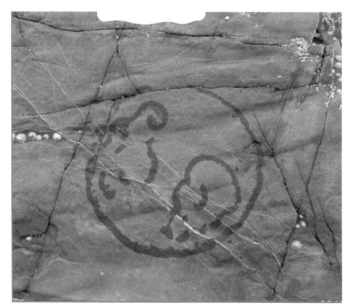

Living in the midst of an ancient monastic settlement at Ross dating back to the 5th century, I had become alert to the possibility of remnants of symbolism referring to the period. Those were the thoughts being provoked by these 'symbolic' markings that I since discovered were entirely natural, ancient and alive in the form of the Green Tar Lichen (*Verrucaria mucosa*). Nothing will persuade me that a message does not exist within this natural sketch!

Early Summer
Sea Pinks(*Armeria maritima*)

Above the tide - Early Summer

At the end of May, above the tide-line is a real treasure trove of flowering flora. Here the **Sea Pinks** have eked out crevices in the soft shale/slate, where silt and other debris has decayed providing a perfect habitat for its long woody root to take hold. The lower shore is in flux with wonderful seaweeds reaching their young growth maturity levels and dangling in unplanned assemblages, each accentuating the features of the others. All the time young molluscs and crustaceans are being recruited into their populations and there is a wonderful sense of life, well being and thriving. Such an assemblage of life cannot be properly worded, but needs to be experienced and felt in the midst of ocean mists and gentle breezes.

Above the lichens - the Saltmarsh

Summer Reeds

Christmas Day

Adding a sense of the terrestrial to the shore at Ross, the abundance and beauty of Summer's verdant plants, especially the ever swishing **Common Reed**, **Red Fescue** grass, and the **Sea Club Rush** is plentiful here. This is the habitat that I refer to as the 'Salt Marsh' normally but not always waterlogged with brackish water, providing a habitat for a significant number of insects, butterflies, worms and birds. To investigate these creatures would require a further immense amount of study and perhaps another publication!. Suffice to realise, that these little creatures all add value to the ecosystem, churning up soils, dispersing seedlings, aiding pollination and generally aiding the diversity of this wild place. During late Autumn the Reeds, Rushes and grasses die back bringing a golden Autumnal touch to the shore.

Above the lichens - the Saltmarsh

One of the pretty Saltmarsh plants is the **Sea Milkwort** (*Glaux maritima*), which begins to bloom here from late May. One can find it still in bloom during July. It lives on thin soils, at the outer edges of the reeds, atop upwardly stratified shale rock, where there is enough provision of soil and water, and along wet tufted embankments of pools of brackish water. It dies back fully in the Autumn. It has dense, oblong fleshy leaves, which turn golden before they die off.

On the edge of the soft muddied land and facing onto the shore, it is the duty of a number of species to dig in deep, intermesh, and protect the edge from coastal erosion. This job is left to plants like **Sea Plantain** (*Plantago maritima*), **Buck's-horn Plantain** (*Plantago coronopus*), **Wild Carrot** (*Daucus carota*), **Wild Thyme** (*Thymus polytrichus*), and **Red Fescue** (*Festuca rubra*). These little holding plants bind the soil, and re-enforce the mud embankment with their penetrating roots. They then face onto the roughest storms, nature has to bring, sometimes they loose the battle as tufts of vegetated earth are flung onto the shoreline.

Top of shore Assemblage

Top of shore Assemblage

At the end of May, a fascinating, colourful, complicated assemblage of rock, gravel, mud, elevation, lichen, flora, seaweed. Just a small patch shows a myriad of micro habitats, and interweaving of plant life from the sea, and plant life from the land. The resurgence and regeneration hosted by Spring growing conditions now evident, with wide ranging plants fully grown and in bloom. The ever present **Gutweed** (*Ulva intestinalatis*) now offering a much brighter yellow green than that of its dull Winter hue. The yellow flowered **Bird's-foot trefoil**, and **Kidney Vetch**, vying for recognition on the coastal edge, while the yellow **Silverweed** spreads itself by its creeping root system along the easy to harrow sandy gravel. This image together with the wondrous spring activities of reproduction and regeneration of seaweeds and creatures down along the shore, presents the elegance and divinity of nature.

7 BEACH COMBING INSIGHTS

Beach Combing, is a traditional practice stretching back through generations and historical coastal communities worldwide. It is an opportunist practice, walking the shoreline to see what may have been beached, something of value, of use, of intrigue, perhaps something to raise alarm amongst the locality. Beach combing by beach hugging communities is therefore necessary and important and also provides opportunity to read the waves, the weather and connect with the ocean.

At Ross Beach and at adjacent Fodera Beach, many historical events unfolded on the shoreline. My mother recalls the life raft landing of survivors from the **Langley Ford** at Fodera Beach, during the early days of the Second World War. This was an English vessel that was torpedoed approximately one hundred and fifty miles west of Loophead, but not before its sailors were given time to vacate it onto life raft. The sailors arrived on shore a week later in very poor condition and one sailor had died. The locals immediately took them onshore and provided them with food and clothing, while the Red Cross services were hailed to move them to hospital. For decades after World War 11, mines and barrels of oil (possibly crude oil, engine oil), arrived at Ross and nearby Fodera Beaches. Controlled explosions were carried out on some of these, which was a source of local human interest. Bales of cotton and rubber found their way to the beach during the War, probably from exploded merchant ships out in the ocean. Such valuable findings were regularly sold onto agents.

At our family level, it was a great tradition to comb the beach, especially first thing in the morning, even before the cows were milked. There was a good reason for this. What landed on Ross beach almost daily were poles of timber - logged wood from Canadian forest felling, that were being transported via downstream river currents to Canadian sawmills or paper mills, some escaped into the Atlantic ocean. These logs together with turf saved at Tullaher Bog, made great fires and provided all our household fuel. Wood was particularly valuable as there are no trees at Loophead, due to its unforgiving exposed territory, leaving a total dearth of this fuel in the area. Wooden poles were often so heavy that they required two to three family members to collect them from the water or low shore and take them to the top of the shore. Bearing in mind these poles may now be festooned with wood worm, they were kept in their own shed, after drying and cutting. This wood was readily available right up until the late 1970s. Nowadays, walking the shoreline, I never encounter such log drift, but I regularly meet small pieces of wood, which used to be referred to as 'cipíns', moulded and rounded somewhat by the oceans own sculpting abilities. I do not know the source of these little wooden pieces, but they two have been collected through the ages, and not just for burning. Many an artist has collected these for their natural and raw beauty incorporating them into artworks and therefore preserving such findings for posterity.

Another reason, we and our neighbours beach combed was to collect 'aluminium and glass seaballs'. These used to be used for marking nets out at sea but were often dragged ashore. These were sold onto agents from time to time. Some locals reused these for flower pots by cutting off the top. Aluminium and glass seaballs have long since been replaced by colourful plastic sea balls with no resale value. Netting was also valuable, and this was used to seal gates, where poultry were kept, make lobster pots for fishing and so forth. These days as I walk the shoreline, netting appears from time to time, especially after ocean turbulence. It is normally entangled in seaweed, Kelps and Thongweed in the Autumn. This and other plastic smithereens, entangled in seaweed, makes the seaweed difficult to remove for soil conditioning, for would be users. At this point in time, removal of beached seaweed for land use or indeed other uses doesn't appear to happen, at least not on any significant scale and is not practiced by beach hugging farmers, who may suggest that is liable to land onto their land during ocean storms all by itself.

There is something intriguing about beach combing, it poses questions, rattles the imagination, and encourages one to think of the bigger picture of the whole wide world embracing the Atlantic ocean.

Beach combing was practiced using unwritten rules by the immediate beach hugging community. A found piece of wood, was often taken up above the tide line to dry out, making it lighter to remove and carry home. Other beach combers did not touch this item, because it had already been found and taken beyond the reach of the ocean. The trick was to be first on the beach at morning time. Sometimes neighbours shared the landings, like the full bale of timber that had over boarded a cargo vessel out at sea. This roofed sheds in the area.

There is a significant difference between 'escaped' log landings and 'dumped' landings. Nowadays, it is possible to find beached 'pallets', probably off-loaded from vessels. These are an eyesore on the beach, as current generations no longer cultivate beach combing opportunities. It is now designated to local community groups, schools and children to clean up, that which the ocean drags in that doesn't belong to the natural order of the shoreline.

Dead wood, a wholly rotten piece of wood, a recent arrival.

Beached netting and other plastics mangled with seaweed makes separation of plastic from seaweed extremely difficult.

October 2011, after Spring tide and ocean storm, a Carribean basket beaches, eventually disappears again. I should have collected it but thought the birds might like it.

This worm festooned 'cipín' would have been collected for firewood. It is now providing a natural habitat for the burrowing worms on the shore.

I can't ever fathom out what's in these barrels. Crude Oil? Engine Oil?

The net-less frame of a Lobster pot. This could be re-used.

8   PULSE EVENTS
An ocean in flux and at war

October 2013

Ross Beach in mid-October 2013, everything orderly, banded, in its place.

O ver the past five years, during the course of this book project I have become intimate with Ross Beach. Like a neat housekeeper who knows where everything is stored, backed up by over six thousand images of this small beach, I was pretty confident, almost to the boulder, of where to find everything. Despite many an ocean storm over the period of this research, there was little change amongst its community of inhabitants. Yes there was beached Kelp and other species, that's a natural selection process. Yes there were movements of shore shingle around the beach generating peaks and throughs especially during Winter months. This didn't greatly change the pattern of life for anyone or anything. Physically and ecologically the beach was banded, aligned and ordered. Approximately fifteen years ago, Clare County Council had installed a **gabion** defense

Jan 4 2014

Jan 12 2014

Jan 12 2014

boundary, to protect the roadside from loose moving shingle being pushed out on occasion by the ocean, especially during rough Spring tides. The gabions had worked well. They contained the beach within the beach, and any spillovers were entirely minimal. Gabions, are wire netted stone boundaries, approx 1 metre -1.2 metres tall and the same breadth and were first designed by Leonardo Da Vinci for the castle foundations of San Marco Castle, in Italy. Gabions saved the adjacent roadside, keeping it open to local and tourist traffic. Before this, the road may have been closed from time to time due to loose flying shingle being pushed off the beach by the elements.

The Summer and Autumn of 2013 were exceptionally warm and mild. Ross Beach was calm throughout the Summer months with little to no beached seaweeds, which was in contrast to the same period of 2012, when there was significant amounts of beached seaweed during the July-September period. Here I am associating beached seaweed with ocean turbulence.

Changes began to set in during December, an unusually windy/stormy month. Due to friction between warm and severe cold fronts far out in the Atlantic Ocean, ocean turbulence set in, as waves rose higher and higher. Coupled with wind power, driving from various western and northerly directions, the ocean was at war. 'Boiling' was a term continuously used by my brother Patrick, who farms adjacent to Ross Beach. It didn't take long for destruction to set in. Storm Catherine was the first storm to blitz a trail of destruction with the new year high tides. It hit every angle of the Peninsula, and surged past all boundaries at Ross beach, driving sea water and ocean rubble including shingle, seaweed and plastic debris four fields deep. It dug large craters in the newly tarmac-ed road rendering it shut to traffic.

Aftermath - The external boundary of the beach and surrounding roads and land has been significantly damaged.

Top left: Not the beach but the fields across the road now showing the oceans expansion, together with its rock and debris. Fields flooded four fields deep in a couple of shore hours from ocean overspill.

Middle left: A newly tar-ed road destroyed. The local community are unable to access, school, church and other facilities.

Bottom left: The gabions, for so long had proved a great protective defense, but on this occasion succumbed to the extreme pressure.

May 2014

Jan 2014

April 2014

I immediately visited the beach after this event. Gulls and Oystercatchers had now moved to the flooded fields, presumably feasting on the myriad of sealife that now found itself landed. It became evident that the Kelp Forest was devasted. This was evidenced by the piles of sea rods on the roads, in the fields, at the top of the beach. With the devastation of the Kelp Forest, came the devastation of a myriad of life forms. I checked several of them, holdfasts laden with eggs, tiny bi-valves commencing life, new growth of red seaweeds like Dillisk along the stipes of the Kelps. None of this life could survive outside its habitat, the relative safety of Kelp Forest. Within the beach, large movements of shingle, rock and boulder have taken place. What was particularly evident was the amount of bedrock that had been 'bitten' off. I use this word because that's what it looked like. Bitten off rock, carrying with them Barnacles, Lichens and other biomass were flung well beyond their location and habitat, turned upside down, a death knell for more shore life.

New expanses of sandy gravel had been opened up on the lower shore, as shingle, small and large had now been flung off beach and onto the road and fields. A new batch of uneven rock found its way into an zone which I used to call the Dead Shell Zone of the beach. Dead Shells were no longer in a congregated zone but rather rendered now invisible.

No part of the inner beach physically escaped, as deep rooted shore plants such as Thrift and Common Reed in the upper Saltmarsh Region were completely uprooted. The ocean facing soft coastal verges are now muddied and lifeless. See page 173 for the same patch of coastline during early Summer 2013.

There are at least four types of bedrock in the Namurian Rock Formation at Ross together with veins of other mineral rock. The formation is deemed to be 300 million years old.

Top Left: The newly changed rock shore scape is evident throughout the shore, with scenes like this.

Corners and slabs of bedrock sandstone complete with living flora and fauna bitten, broken and cast off site.

Soft edge of land in mid-April which would normally be verdant and inhabited by a mixed variety of coastal flora see page 173 for a typical example .

29 Jan 2014

I was therefore more than surprised that on surveying the shore gastropod community, Winkles, Limpets, Whelks, that it appeared very much business as usual, the day after the storm. The tiniest of brightly coloured baby **Flat Periwinkles** attached to the fronds of **Carrigeen** on dark lower shore pools. Juvenile **Edible Periwinkles** openly grazing rock surfaces in what looked like regular numbers. The **Common Dog Whelk** is found up to its regular predatory behaviour, and whilst a number of larger Limpets appear to have been knocked off their lower shore rocks and perhaps lost to the storm, nonetheless, the new baby Limpets that are born during the rough Winter months have held their tiny positions both on open rock surfaces, in crevices and throughout their range throughout the shore. The size of these creatures at this time is approx 6-8mm. They receive no parental care. This is good news, life goes on. A further investigation of the Anemones, shows that despite their soft bodies due to a lack of a hard shell, they appear in good number and unharmed. I may have encountered one that showed damage, perhaps hit by a flying boulder. In the few pools where James and I had been monitoring an inward and upward movement of the **Elegant Anemone** over a number of years, and having watched them all during Christmas, I am happy to report, they are still there, in their regular numbers and alive.

The story of the seashore and its inhabitants is an intriguing one. How can such tiny creatures, hold on, evade, hide from a flooding powerful turbulence that practically left no stone unturned and hurtled everything in sight? While so much millions of life was lost by the loss of the Kelp Forest here, the magic remains that so many tiny creatures survived without apparent trauma.

02 Feb 2014

Above left: The January storms swung lower shore shingle to new heights creating a temporary gravelly space at the front of the shore.

Middle left: Storm Bridget on Feb 1, left a ' mud bared beach' as all the loose shingle was flung far and wide beyond its boundary.

Bottom Left: Ross Beach always contained a **Dead Shell Zone**, a particular sandy gravel part of the beach with a myriad of dead shells which we enjoyed collecting for generations. This zone has disappeared without a trace.

Oct 2011

4 Jan 2014

12 Jan 2014

12 Jan 2014

Storm Catherine was succeeded by several more vicious storms that attacked the same coastline. **Storm Bridget** on February 1st, one month after Storm Catherine, was the third such major storm. Accompanied by a Spring Tide, it reeked havoc on a scale far beyond that of Storm Catherine. The road that had been re-opened was smashed to a degree that six weeks later, it remains closed. The protective gabions were plunged out onto the road as the ocean suggested it required more space. The lovely orderly lines that presented on the shore and its boundary, last October are now in disarray. Continuous recording between storms have shown a continuous physical movement within the beach of smooth shingle, rough shingle, broken off bed rock and the soft margins that faced onto the beach from the eastern side have been left muddied and vulnerable as the Red Fescue and other deep rooted plants were dragged off.

Down on the shallow sub-tidal, where the larger seaweeds like **Sugar Kelp, Forest Kelp, Tangle Weed** grow profusely, there is evidence of huge loss together with remaining plants looking like they were bitten off from below the meristem, suggesting that there may be no regeneration possible for the feeble stipes that now stand vertical and headless in the water. There was no evidence of regeneration six weeks later. In the absence of all this egg laying surface for sea slugs, some have laid their eggs on the stipes of these Kelps, especially the Sugar Kelp and the Tangle Kelp. Another fascinating discovery during my after storm visits was to discover that eggs laid by sea slugs on the open fronds of Sugar Kelps that were saved, were still in position, held by a mucus coating, like a glue, the day after the pulse event.

Top Left: Deep roots of **Common Reed** torn up.

Middle Left: just one of hundreds of broken off pieces of ancient bedrock from the upper splash zone of the beach, laden with lichen, and tumbled into a new location.

Bottom left: Throughout the splash zone, which is the **Lichen** living area of the beach, ancient slow growing Lichens have been beaten off their host rock leaving blank spaces.

March 2014

The large stipes of **Tangle Kelp** that remained in the sub-tidal showed that they looked like they were bitten off.

There were other seaweeds that survived intact. The very tough **Serrated Wrack**, that lives through Winter and has a discoid holdfast heavily cemented onto bedrock and boulder, survived pretty much in tact. As this wrack provides a home to a myriad of creatures such as coiled tube worms, ascidians and egg mass, I contend it is one of the safest surfaces on which to set up base. Seaweeds like **Carrigeen** survived well on the lower shore boulders, and the biggest seaweed loss was no doubt the Kelps. It will be interesting to note if there will be a changing pattern in species balance in the coming months and years, as faster settling species, like **Furbellows Kelp** may take over where Forest Kelp thought it could survive.

Top left: Life goes on in a rocky shore as in the midst of the storms, sea slugs, like the **Banded Chink Shell** *(Lacuna vincta)* continue their reproduction process by laying large quantities of egg capsules on the fronds and stipes of the Kelps. There is no doubt that this sea slug would have preferred a broad fronded kelp on which to lay its eggs, perhaps the same location is chosen annually. Now it has left them on an exposed stipe.

Bottom left: On examination of several Kelps, especially the holdfast and stipes, I find a whole array of life that is now left to die in fields, on fences by the road side, no hope of reconnecting with the turbulent ocean, no hope of surviving. Providing rich pickings for coastal birds.

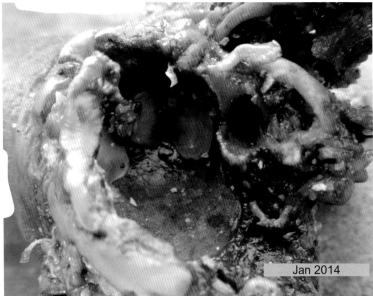

Jan 2014

01 Mar 2014

02 Feb

The huge disturbance and loss to the shallow sub-tidal can be seen in this image taken the day after **Storm Bridge**t. Much of what's left standing are the broken stipes of **Tangle Kelp**, its holdfast may have proved stronger holding than that of the Forest Kelp, and in any case its stipe is more flexible. There is little hope for re-generation here due to the breakage occurring too low down the seaweed.

Left - Mud ball shaped carving remains among the remaining shingle after Storm Bridget. Circular carving by the ocean.

FINAL WORDS

The journey of making this book is nearing its end. It has been a few months of finally pulling the layers, segments, detail and story of Ross Beach into a sense of logical order for the ultimate reader. I have sifted through more than 6000 photos of the beach time and again, not just to present the best of them herewith but to browse them as evidence to back up the story of the beach and its inhabitants.

I grew up within a stones throw of this place, but really I had to be led here. In the early days it was young James, my son, researching for his Sherkin Island Marine Station, Environmental competition project, who encouraged me along. This is a great way of encouraging children into the natural environment and Sherkin have been providing this opportunity for some decades now. It didn't take long to overwhelm me. James spent the first couple of years with me, providing a sense of company, beyond the closure of his projects and then took a break. At this point I didn't need company anymore, for I had by now enlisted all the company that the shore had to provide.

Being in the midst of Ross beach, Loophead all of my life, and finally presenting myself with the opportunity to take a deep study of it has afforded me the privilege of a lifetime. I cannot possibly describe in words, the exquisite journey into the realm of the rocky shore world that unfolded. For the first time in my life, my eyes were wholly engaged with consuming detail, from a wild natural world. Questions asked, some answered, some remain in the realms of mystery. We picked up on interesting movements, like those of the Elegant Anemone (*Sagartia elegans*), that had heretofore received no textbook coverage in relation to their movements. After a number of years and as my quest for detail became more defined at the species level, I stumbled upon their tiny babies in development mode on heavily covered Carrigeen rocks on the extreme lower shore. This was palpable moment of joy.

To me, Ross Beach has become the most fascinating place on earth. My work here seemed completely natural to me, like I was engaged by a higher order to do this work. This book was written by nature itself, I being a simple conduit in the process.

The rocky shore is art, pure living art. The images of assemblages throughout this book bear testament to this. The movements, densities, species, textures, in their various combinations, infuse my artwork and indeed, have done so long before my more recent exposures to these assemblages. The rocky shore is wild and expressive, so too are my artworks laden with energy, carefree, moving. This is the source of the inspiration and the artistic interpretation.

I believe Irish people have not engaged or properly appreciated their coastline since the Famine era. As the Famine era came to an end, coastal folk shied away from the shoreline associating it with extreme poverty. Indeed the shore kept many alive during the Famine, even if they had neither the know how or means to make tasty dishes with its offerings. Times have changed, and education and study have replaced this humble era. It is now time to reconnect with the shoreline, for its entire package, amenity, knowledge building, intrigue, diversity, edible offerings, opportunity, fresh air and connections with the wild world. As a country with 2600kms of coastline, I believe we should make better use of it across the above spectrum. I believe our National Authorities need to assist in the education of our coastal communities. Education and opportunity development in this respect needs to be delivered right on the edge.

Generations will come and go and Ross Beach will radically, if quietly change both ecologically and physically through time. Here as with all life forms, the only constant is change. This book serves as a record in time and space, a record that may be referred to as climate change, ecological mix and physical ocean pressures are each brought to bear on its address at the North East Atlantic rocky shoreline at Ross Beach, Loophead, Mid-Western Irish Coastline.

ACKNOWLEDGEMENTS

This book could not have been born without the positive encouragement provided by so many people who support my work in many ways. Trying to get everyone included here is indeed futile.

Most especially, this book would have remained on the beach unwritten but for the re-connection with the beach that was brokered by Master James Madigan. The thrill and joy of our numerous adventurous trips together at low tide drove the research well into three years. James was in turn encouraged and appreciated by his school, Barefield National School, and driven by the excitement of presenting a lovely rocky shore project to Sherkin Island for their Environmental Competition each year. Winning these three times propelled us both.

It's amazing how small nuggets of encouragement can yield exponential results. We all need positive encouragement. Always nudging and encouraging this book to be written were John and Margaret Burns, Mary Gibson, Conjella Maguire, Bridie Davis, Mai & PJ Magner, Patrick & Mary Magner(where the kettle was always on after my trips to the beach), Mary Tevlin, Joan Keating, Peter Madigan, James Madigan, Sr. Mary O' Connell.

On a broader scale, the positive support provided by individuals and organizations towards my work and Hedge School set up were very welcome and indeed much needed. I would therefore like to thank the Heritage Council, Matt Murphy, Sherkin Island Marine Station, Department of Education, Kevin O' Sullivan, Irish Times, Michael Viney, Paddy Woodward, Zoe Devlin, Dr. Stephen Ward, Jenny Walshe Bassett, Dr. Fidelma Butler, UCC, Clare Education Centre, OPW, The Clare Champion, National Biodiversity Data Centre, Fergal Madigan, Clare Local Development Company, all the participants of my Hedge School Modules during 2012 and 2013, Loophead Tourism, Kilballyowen Development Company, Clare People, Noirín Buckley, Paul O' Donoghue, Ann Carmody, Josephine Glynn, extended Madigan family, extended Magner Family. Clare Arts Office, Susan Naughton, various parishioners and school friends Kilballyowen & Barefield, Clare FM, Barefield National School, Cross National School.

I would like to thank Dr. John Breen, Dept. of Life Sciences, University of Limerick for reading through the book, and offering very valuable suggestions, Matt Murphy, Sherkin Island Marine Station for browsing the book and fore-wording the book and for practical advice, Master James Madigan, for his entertaining Foreword, Michael Viney for browsing the book and offering lovely feedback. I would like to thank Robert Madigan for his lovely sketches on page 7, Seasearch Identifications on Facebook for assisting with a few identities, Irish Seaweed Research Centre for assisting with a few seaweed identities, Seasearch author Chris Wood and Irish Seaweed Kitchen Author, Dr. Prannie Rhattigan for her positivity and enthusiastically agreeing to launch this book.

Finally and most importantly, this book has been completely financed by the Madigan Family. This book would therefore have remained unpublished, even if fully written without the surefooted intervention of my husband, Peter Madigan, who insisted that such a book needed publication. This was indeed a generous contribution to the rich natural coastal heritage of Loophead and the North East Atlantic Irish coastline a record in time and space, for present and future generations and scientists to access, study and appreciate, and a fervent belief in my work.

Thank you Peter.

BIBLIOGRAPHY

Little Colin, Williams Gray A., Trowbridge Cynthia D. 'The Biology of Rocky Shores' 2010 - Oxford University Press

Rosenfeld, Ann Wertheim, with Paine Robert T. ' The Intertidal Wilderness' 2002 - University of California Press

Dobson, Frank S. ' A Field Key to Coastal and Seashore Lichens' - 2010 - Frank D. Dobson

Sherkin Island Marine Station, Kay Paul, 'Ireland's Hidden Depths' - 2011 - Sherkin Island Marine Station

Rhatigan, Prannie, 'Irish Seaweed Kitchen' - 2009 - Booklink

Wood Chris - Sea Anemones & Corals of Britain and Ireland - 2013 - Seasearch Publications

Bunker, Francis Stp, Brodie, Juliet A., Maggs, Christine A, Bunker, Anne R. ' Guide to Seaweeds of Britain and Ireland' - 2010 - Seasearch Publications

Murphy, John N. 'Birds of Fanore' 2013 The Burren & Cliffs of Moher Geopark & John N. Murphy

Cummins Valerie, Coughlan, Susan, McClean Orla, Connolly Niamh, Mercer John, Burnell Gavin ' An Assessment of the potential for the sustainable development of the Edible Periwinkle, *Littorina littorea*, Industry in Ireland - 2002 CMRC - Coastal & Marine Resource Centre UCC

Werner Astrid, Dring Matthew - 'Aquaculture Explained - Cultivating *Palmaria palmata*' 2011 - BIM - Bord Iascaigh Mhara

Stanley Norman, 'Production & Utilization of products from Commercial Seaweeds' FMC Corporation - Marine Colloids Division

Kelly, Dr. Eamonn, ' The Role of Kelp in the Marine Environment' - 2005 - National Parks & Wildlife Service

Bruton Tom, ' A Review of the potential of Marine Algae as a source of Biofuel in Ireland' - 2009 SEI - Sustainable Energy Ireland

Edwards Maeve, Watson Lucy - ' Aquaculture Explained - Cultivating *Laminaria digitata*'- BIM - Bord Iascaigh Mhara

Werner Astrid, Dring Matthew - Development and Demonstration of viable hatchery and ongrowing methodologies for seaweed species with identified commercial potential' 2011 - BIM

Sherkin Island Marine Station 'A Beginners Guide to the Seashore' 2010 - Sherkin Island Marine Station

Iselin Josie 'An Ocean Garden - The Secret Life of Seaweed' - 2013 - Abrams Books

Braune, Guiry, 'Seaweeds' 2011 - Koeltz Books

Local Action Group West (FLAG) BIM - 2013 'Strategy for the Sustainable Development of Fishery Dependent Communities, Galway & Clare' - Fisheries (FLAG - BIM)

Walsh Máirtín ' Seaweed Harvesting in Ireland' - 2012 - BIM

BIBLIOGRAPHY contd.

Tait R.V, Dipper F.A, 'Elements of Marine Ecology' - 1998 - Butterworth Heinemann

Doyle Tom, Murphy Ailish, 'Jellyfish in our Coastal Seas' - The Heritage Council

Miller Frederic P., Vandome Agnes F., McBrewster John, 'Coastal Management' - 2009 - Alphascript Publishing

Websites:

marlin.ac.uk
seaweeds.ie
algaebase.org
fishkilkee.ie
kilkeethalasso.com
seasearch.org.uk
marine.ie
seaweedindustry.com
heritagecouncil.ie
biodiversityireland.ie
met.ie
npws.ie
coastalheritage.ie
worldweatheronline.com
newfoundlandlabrador.com - Tourism
http://ngb.chebucto.org/Articles/kc (Newfoundland Grand Banks Site)
Facebook.com/Kings Cove NL
facebook.com/NewfoundlandLabradorTourism
Loophead.ie

INDEX